This book is dedicated to the artists whose talents have enriched our lives and to Alice Lighthall, C.J.G. Molson and James Houston who had the vision and courage to make it all possible.

1. COVER:
UNIDENTIFIED ARTIST
Sugluk
1955
stone
26.5 x 19.0 x 15.0
133.

GUILDE   CANADIAN

CANADIENNE   GUILD

DES MÉTIERS D'ART   OF CRAFTS

QUÉBEC   QUEBEC

THE PERMANENT COLLECTION

INUIT ARTS AND CRAFTS

C.1900-1980

ISBN 0-9690591-1-6

Photography — Charlie King

Design and Editorial — Virginia J. Watt

Colour Separation — Hadwen Graphics/Ottawa

Typesetting and Printing — Dollco Printing/Ottawa

Published by Canadian Guild of Crafts Quebec

CONTENTS

PATRONS

Claudia Ferguson

Hudson's Bay Company

R.T. La Prairie

Alice M.S. Lighthall, CM

C.J.G. Molson, CM

Constance V. Pathy

Phoenix Natural Science Association

W.J. Piper

Dorothy M. Stillwell

P. McG. Stoker

Virginia J. Watt

ACKNOWLEDGEMENTS

The preparation of this book involved the help of many people. The research and documentation of the collection began in 1976 and was completed in 1980. I wish to acknowledge the cooperation which I received from many of the artists who identified their works; and from Deborah Feinstein, Diana Borso, Terence Ryan and Peter Murdoch for their assistance.

I would like to express my sincere appreciation to Marybelle Myers, Helga Goetz and William E. Taylor, Jr. for their splendid essays.

Also, I wish to thank Olga Burman and Nairy Kalemkerian for their patience in typing the documentation and text.

This book could not have been published without the interest and the encouragement of our Patrons. I wish to extend my deepest gratitude to them for their generous support.

Virginia J. Watt
Managing Director
Canadian Guild of Crafts Quebec
1980.

All measurements are given in centimeters in the following order: height, width, depth.

FOREWORD

There are collections one raves about, or that some rave about, and there are those everyone should know about regardless of ravings. The Canadian Guild of Crafts collection earns the raves indeed, and all concerned with Canadian Inuit art should be familiar with it. It is a thoroughly enjoyable experience because in part, so many artists are represented.

The range of places, the time span, the variety of media and topics increase the merit of this collection in which distinctive pieces abound. Especially attractive are the small and earlier pieces which delight one, capture the eye and provoke thoughts of the culture, the attitudes, the thinking that produced these sculptures. It all comes from the mind and hand of the Inuit.

The collection totals a refreshing review of recent Inuit art and constitutes a distinguished tribute and an elegant witness to a remarkable people.

William E. Taylor, Jr.
Director
National Museum of Man
Ottawa

THE BEGINNING

"The first exhibition of Eskimo Art took place in Montreal at the Canadian Handicrafts Guild[1] in 1949. The exhibition was sold out in three days."

This news item has been reprinted many times in newspapers, magazines, promotional material and books. In 1977, a clipping service provided me with 23 copies of this statement from 23 Canadian newspapers. My intent here is not to editorialize on the cause or the effect of this news story but rather to relate the events which preceded the exhibition in 1949 and the four years which followed.

The Canadian Handicrafts Guild was founded in 1906 as a non-profit organization. Its aims and objectives were as follows:

1. To encourage, retain, revise and develop Canadian Handicrafts and Art Industries throughout the Dominion.
2. To prevent loss, extinction and deterioration of the same.
3. To encourage home industry by making it profitable and honourable.
4. To aid people skilled in such crafts and industries by providing markets for their products in Canada and abroad.
5. To educate the public as to the value of such arts, industries and crafts.

The Guild was a national organization with its headquarters in Montreal. Over the years it developed branch organizations in other cities throughout Canada. Among the first members of the Guild were people who had collections of Indian and Eskimo[2] crafts. It is not surprising that one of the Guild's interests was to encourage the native peoples of Canada to produce good traditional crafts. Guild members organized exhibitions and competitions for the Indian people. They produced travelling shows, some of which included Eskimo crafts which they borrowed for the occasions from private collectors.

In 1930 the Guild organized an exhibition of Eskimo Arts and Crafts at the McCord Museum in Montreal. The artifacts and small ivory carvings captured the imagination of the public and press alike. It isn't usual for the New York Times to review an exhibition held in Montreal, but this one drew the paper's comments.[3] There were several attempts made by the Hudson's Bay Company during the great depression years of the thirties to encourage and develop an Eskimo craft market but none were successful.

In March 1939, the Indian Committee of the Guild *"moved duly seconded that the Indian Committee's name be changed to Indian and Eskimo Committee and that its scope be extended to include the encouragement of Eskimo work".[4]* Miss Alice Lighthall was chairman of the committee and among its twelve members were Dr. Diamond Jenness and Major David McKeand of the Northwest Territories Administration Office. Major McKeand had reported to the Guild that poor hunting years in the North caused acute suffering and deprivation among the people and that this condition might be alleviated by developing a market for Eskimo crafts in the South. The following year he sent a small collection of crafts which he had obtained while on an inspection tour of the Ungava, with the request that the Guild should *"take up the work of encouraging Eskimo handicrafts through white women now in the Arctic."[5]*

The Committee's assessment of this collection reads as follows: *"There are among them some curious and clever attempts to imitate articles of daily use .... miniature baskets and a kerosene lamp, complete with chimney. We hope there may be an opportunity to direct some of these efforts along simpler and more practical lines! ..... the function of this Committee in relation to (native) products, must continue to be in the encouragement of the best use of traditional design, material and workmanship and the education of an appreciative and discerning public."[6]*

In 1939 the Guild had exhibited a collection on loan from the Right Reverend A.L. Fleming, Bishop of the Arctic. The exhibition included *"very fine Eskimo fur work and walrus tusk ivories. Especially fine is the great seal altar frontal made by the women of Pangnirtung for the new Cathedral at Aklavik".[7]*

The Montreal members of the committee met and drew up a tentative plan with suggestions for a leaflet to be distributed to *"anyone on the ground anxious to take part in the effort".* Dr. Jenness arranged for the committee to meet in Ottawa where specimens from the Museum Collection could be used to illustrate the discussion. Miss Lighthall reported, *"In a detailed discussion of the whole matter — the possibilities of developing existing skills, directing them to the use of native materials and designs rather than to borrowed ones and the question of marketing the products — many interesting points were brought out. The art of basketry, for instance, is only practised among the Eastern Eskimo of a limited district in the Ungava. It was taught to them by Moravian missionaries about 200 years ago."*[8]

A leaflet was prepared asking for the recipients' cooperation and suggesting that small competitions could be held to encourage good work. Major McKeand was to undertake the distribution of the leaflet which would cover *"every post where there was a missionary, nurse, teacher, wife of a Hudson's Bay Factor or a member of the R.C.M.P.".* What the results were of this plan are not recorded. We do know that the Guild's efforts in the Arctic were severely curtailed during the Second World War. Seven years later the plan was revised and put into action.

In 1947 the Guild had been informed that small stone carvings were being made in the Ungava and the Guild was asked to do everything in its power to encourage this work. Hunting was poor and the people were in desperate need of an additional income. Colonel P.B. Baird, Director of the Montreal office of the Arctic Institute of North America was a new member of the Guild's Indian and Eskimo Committee. He agreed to supply a list of names of white women, living in the Arctic who would be willing to encourage and stimulate the production of good crafts.[9] A letter written by Miss Lighthall, outlined the Guild's objectives and expressed concern that the rapid invasion of the North by white people could have a derogatory effect on the special skills of the northern people. She emphasized the need to encourage the independence and individuality of the craftsmen. The letter was sent to 25 women in the following communities: Arctic Bay, Cape Smith, Fort Chimo, Pangnirtung, Port Harrison (Inoucdjouac), Povungnituk, Southampton Island, Sugluk, Baker Lake, Great Whale River, Chesterfield Inlet, Eskimo Point and Pond Inlet. A list of suggestions accompanied the letter. The preface to the list is worth repeating: *"The native work of the Eskimo is unique in the world to-day. It is a survival of the crafts that were carried on by very early man. In any work we do with the Eskimo, it would be well to remember this and that we should encourage them to use their own materials and methods rather than to imitate ours. We have the responsibility of not*

letting them forget their own arts".[10] Alice Lighthall was indeed, the right woman at the right time.

The following is a direct quote from the minutes of the Indian and Eskimo Committee meeting of November 18, 1948: *"Mr. J.A. Houston of Grandmère who visited Port Harrison during the past summer spoke to the committee at some length about his plan to encourage craft work among the Eskimos of that district. Mr. Houston felt very strongly that the latent skills of the Eskimos could be brought forth if there was someone on the spot to encourage them. He gave the names of Miss Woodrow and Miss Andrews, two white women in Port Harrison, who had asked him if he could return next summer and help them in this work. Mr. Houston asked for the co-operation of the Guild through the Hudson's Bay Company whose stores would perhaps be able to arrange to supply food in return for pieces of good craft work".* The meeting continued with a lengthy discussion about ways and means of transporting finished work, standards of craftsmanship and the types of crafts produced in the area. *"The Guild agreed to sponsor Mr. Houston in his effort to promote the production of crafts in and around Port Harrison and Povungnituk."* James Houston was the right man at the right time.

The Indian and Eskimo Committee was a group of volunteers, without funds but endowed with unquenchable enthusiasm. They met with Mr. C.J.G. Molson who was then President of the Quebec Branch of the Canadian Handicrafts Guild. He agreed to the proposal that the Quebec Branch Shop provide the funds for the proposed test-purchase at Port Harrison which Mr. Houston would undertake during the summer of 1949. *"$1100. had been underwritten by the shop and placed to the credit of Houston at the Hudson's Bay Company. Travelling expenses were estimated at $400."*[11]

In the context of 1980, $1500. is a very small amount of money, but in 1949 to a non-profit craft organization without access to any funding other than what they earned in their shop, the expenditure of $1500. on the unknown, is a courageous and daring act. It is noted that on December 31, 1948, the Quebec Shop recorded a loss for twelve months of $467.[12]

The Guild received a letter in July 1949 from Mr. R.A. Gibson, Deputy Commissioner of the Northwest Territories Administration Office *"asking about the extent of our work and plans for the Eskimo".* Miss Lighthall went to Ottawa to have an interview. *"Mr. Gibson said that Mr. Houston's activities had been reported to the Administration by the R.C.M.P. Inspector, and that the matter interested them considerably. The N.W.T. Administration had decided to expand handicrafts work for the Eskimo, especially in view of the polio victims whose lifelong support must be considered. They had already appointed four teachers for the*

Eastern Arctic, whose work would begin in the fall. .... The organization proposed by the Department was to start with a committee composed of government and lay members, in which they wished to include a representative of the Guild. They would like also that the Guild's Indian and Eskimo Committee include a representative of the Department, Mr. James G. Wright."[13]
The Committee agreed to invite Mr. Wright to join them.

In October, Mr. Wright was invited to speak to the Committee about the Government's plans. He reported the problems which had been brought about by the depressed price of furs and that *"the Department of Mines and Resources was looking forward to securing the services of a man who would organize the whole new handicraft industry among the Eskimo, but the appointment of this official had not yet been made. Miss Lighthall mentioned that the Handicrafts Division of the Department of Indian Affairs had taken quantity rather than quality in their Indian handicraft products and thus they are losing their distinctive market. It was pointed out that the same thing should not happen to the Eskimo craft market."*[14] When a suggestion was made to teach art in the northern schools, Miss Lighthall advised the speaker to *"send the children to their grandfathers for that"*. The meeting concluded with a suggestion from Mr. Wright that a letter should be written to Mr. R.A. Gibson requesting a Government grant *"so that the Guild should continue its worthy work among the Eskimos."*[15] In early November, James Houston was appointed the *"Canadian Handicrafts Guild's Arctic Representative"*. Plans were made to apply for a Government grant so that Mr. Houston's work could be expanded to include other areas in the Arctic. November 21, 1949 was the date set for the exhibition and sale of the works collected in the Port Harrison area during the previous summer.[16]

In May 1950, Mr. Molson reported that *"The Government grant of $8000. had been received."*[17] The grant was given to cover costs of travel and salary for James Houston for two years.

At a meeting at the Guild in October 1950, Miss Lighthall reported as follows: *"Mr. Houston made two trips to the Arctic. The first trip extended from the 1st of March to the middle of July 1950, and covered the Port Harrison area on the East coast of Hudson's Bay. The second trip extended from early August to the latter part of September and covered the West coast of Hudson's Bay. In the Port Harrison, Povungnituk and Cape Smith area the quality of handicrafts was found to be greatly improved over that of the previous summer. The Guild is receiving the utmost cooperation from the Hudson's Bay Company and it is recommended that a letter of thanks be written to Mr. R.H. Chesshire. The Royal Canadian Mounted Police offered to carry (transport) crates of handicrafts — some of these, unfortunately have been damaged by sea water and storms. Total purchases of $6200. have been authorized to date in this area. Purchases on the West coast were comparatively small, as Mr. Houston did not find much available handicraft work there.*

He expects that better results will be produced in 1951. He was prevented by ice from covering Igloolik. In Chesterfield Inlet where he had gone at the request of the Government to work with the Eskimo polio victims, he was unable to work due to the fact that food and accommodation were not made available. $300. worth of crafts were purchased in Repulse Bay and $600. was left with the Manager of the Hudson's Bay Post in order that he might continue to purchase and to inform the Guild when that amount should be increased."[18]
Miss Lighthall noted that sales of the Eskimo articles were proceeding satisfactorily through the Canadian Handicrafts Shop, its agents and exhibitions. At the same meeting, Mr. Molson read an estimate of expenses which he had prepared in connection with the application for renewal of the Government grant for 1951. This grant was to cover a period of seven months of travel in Baffin Island and the Ungava for two people. (Mr. Houston was about to be married). The items on the list included: files, emery paper, needles, beads, boxes, dog team travel, arctic tent, winter clothing, food, sleeping bags, primus stove, insurance, etc. Other than salaries, the most expensive item was dog team travel at $600. The estimate totalled $8000.[19] The Guild's "Eskimo Project" net profit for the year ending December 31, 1950 was $167.[20]

The Houstons' trip to the Arctic in 1951 was successful. They visited Lake Harbour, Cape Dorset, Frobisher Bay, Pangnirtung, Clyde River, Pond Inlet and Sugluk. They reported that the travelling had been good on sea and ice and that *"they had been helped by the Eskimos everywhere".*[21] About 2000 carvings and crafts had been purchased on Baffin Island with the cooperation of the Hudson's Bay Company store managers. 58 cases had arrived at the Guild with the balance expected on the next trip of the "C.D. Howe". There would also be shipments from the Hudson's Bay Posts in the Ungava.

During 1950 the Guild had organized Eskimo Art exhibitions in Toronto, Calgary and New York. In 1951, this program was expanded and exhibitions were sent to the National Gallery of Canada and the Royal Ontario Museum. Stories of the exhibitions and the Arctic adventures of the Houstons were reported in Canadian Geographic, Vogue, Canadian Art, Time and Life magazines. Requests for radio interviews with the Houstons were frequent. The public was enchanted with this new, curious and exotic art form.

The Guild was faced with the problem of having to finance the ever increasing flow of shipments from the north, months before the goods were received in Montreal. Skins and furs which had not been properly cured had to be destroyed. Carvings and crafts that were not up to standard were not offered for sale. Breakage was a common and costly problem. The exhibition and sale of November 1952 had been disappointing and efforts were made to stimulate markets in other parts of Canada and in the United States.[22] Preparations were made for an exhibition in 1953 at Gimpel Fils in London, England during the time of the Coronation. Mr. Houston made arrangements with Mr. Eugene B. Power of Ann Arbour, Michigan to supply the American market through the Guild. Mr. Molson reported in May 1953 that *"the opening of new markets both here and in the United States looked promising."*[23]

Throughout all of the early years the Hudson's Bay Company and the Guild worked in close cooperation. The Company's assistance in the Arctic to James and Alma Houston was invaluable. In 1953, the Guild could no longer continue to purchase the entire production from the Eastern Arctic. An agreement was made with the Hudson's Bay Company that *"the Company would handle all the direct buying from the Eskimo and that the Guild would purchase its allotment from them."*[24]

In James Houston's report of his trip to the Eastern Arctic in the summer of 1953 he states *"Eskimo handicrafts show a marked improvement in 10 of the 12 separate areas where they are now being purchased by the Guild."* He mentions in particular Port Harrison where *"Norman Ross and R. Ploughman of the Hudson's Bay Company have done much to encourage all of the carvers and as a result can show splendid work from a great many rather than a few."*[25]

Mr. Molson received a letter in August 1953 from Mr. H.A. Young, Deputy Minister of the Department of Resources and Development, Ottawa. The letter stated *"that arrangements are underway to increase the scope of the Arctic Services Section of the Northern Administration and Lands Branch. The development of the handicrafts industry is one of several projects we have in mind ....."*. The letter went on to say that the Government would establish vocational and training centres at Aklavik and Frobisher Bay where instruction in trades and crafts would be given and that *"in view of the decision of the department to assume the expenses of and the direct responsibility for field work, I have been brought reluctantly to the conclusion that the annual grant the department has made to the Guild in the past for handicraft work among the Eskimo will have to be discontinued. This decision in no way reflects the work the Guild has done in developing handicrafts in the Eastern Arctic."* The letter concluded with the hope that the Guild *"will give the department your continued support and advice ... and we hope to have your continued cooperation in developing outlets ..."*.[25] Mr. Molson's reply thanked the writer for his letter and said

"we will therefore plan our activities in accordance with the changed circumstances."[26] He warned the Government of the dangers of mass production and stated that the Guild would continue to co-operate with the Government in the marketing of *"Eskimo arts and crafts of high quality"*.

The Government's decision was a blow to the Guild but not for long. Miss Lighthall with exceptional resilience wrote to Mr. Molson *"that the Government's decision was not without its brighter side. .... We welcome the news that they are planning other projects for the Eskimo, thereby releasing the unnatural strain put upon handicrafts to replace relief in times of hardship."*[27] Miss Lighthall recommended that *"we should urge the Government to put its energies into developing general and scientific education among the people, making practical installations to help their economy and leave the arts alone."*[28]

By the end of the fifties the Inuit Cooperative movement had started in the north. Today, the cooperatives own and operate their own distribution agencies in the south. The Hudson's Bay Company continues to distribute carvings purchased by their northern store managers.

The years of 1949-1953 were years of an experiment without precedent. No one knew then whether the project would succeed or fail. These years were the beginning of what is today a multi-million dollar Inuit enterprise.

Notes

1. The name was changed in 1967 to Canadian Guild of Crafts.
2. The term "Inuit" is in common usage today.
3. December 14, 1930.
4. Indian and Eskimo Committee Minutes March 17, 1939.
5. Canadian Handicrafts Guild Annual Meeting 1939.
6. Ibid.
7. Canadian Handicrafts Guild Annual Meeting 1940
8. Ibid.
9. Indian and Eskimo Committee Minutes April 8, 1948.
10. July 12, 1948.
11. Canadian Handicrafts Guild Quebec Branch, Shop Committee meeting April 7, 1949. The Quebec Branch became autonomous in 1967. The name was changed to Canadian Guild of Crafts Quebec.
12. Auditor's report for the year ending December 31, 1948.

13. Canadian Handicrafts Guild, Meeting of the Board of Directors, October 4, 1949.
14. Indian and Eskimo Committee Minutes October 25, 1949.
15. Ibid.
16. Quebec Branch Shop Committee Minutes October 26, 1949.
17. Ibid. Minutes May 11, 1950.
18. Indian and Eskimo Committee Minutes October 26, 1950.
19. Ibid.
20. Indian and Eskimo Committee Minutes January 29, 1951.
21. Quebec Branch Shop Committee Minutes October 18, 1951.
22. Ibid. Minutes December 3, 1952.
23. Ibid. Minutes May 11, 1953.
24. Ibid.
25. Ibid. Minutes October 22, 1953.
26. August 17, 1953.
27. August 21, 1953.
28. Ibid.
29. Ibid.

Virginia J. Watt
1980.

THE COLLECTION

One of the most distinguished collections of Inuit art is that of the Canadian Guild of Crafts. Its excellence and breadth reflect the discriminating judgement and continued support of a group of individuals responsible for introducing Inuit art to the Canadian public.

The collection ranges from small, anonymous ivory carvings from the early part of this century to major works of well-known contemporary sculptors. It contains numerous interesting examples of fine handicrafts and a small collection of graphics including a special lithograph commissioned from Cape Dorset artist Pudlo Pudlat in celebration of thirty years of the Guild's involvement in the promotion of Inuit art.

Carvings from the period 1950-1965 form the nucleus of the collection but a lesser quantity of high quality works continues to be added. Geographic distribution is greatest from Cape Dorset, Inoucdjouac and Povungnituk, as these areas were the most productive during the period of intense collecting.

Representations of traditional Inuit life predominate over more abstract or decorative carvings, reflecting the special interest of Guild members in native culture. The majority are small to moderate in size, ranging from 2.5 to 42.0 centimetres. A high percentage are of exceptional quality.

Overall, the collection is one in which Inuit artists and Guild members alike can take enormous pride. To highlight a few of the works will, I hope, provide stimulation for the reader to view the collection in its many aspects.

Kiawak Ashoona of Cape Dorset is a major sculptor active for the past twenty-five years. He is represented by a number of works including the graceful sedna figure featured on a recent Canadian postage stamp (16). Sedna, or Tallilao, the woman who rules over the creatures of the sea is a central figure in Inuit mythology and a popular subject for carvings and graphics. Cape Dorset artists often show her as a playful, sensuous creature. Kiawak's representation is a typical example. He shows her braiding her hair, the finished plait looped over her fish-like tail. The highly polished local green stone complements the curving shape of the woman-fish.

Kiawak's carving of a bear with human face (5) reflects the traditional cultural belief in the possibility of transformation from human to animal form. People with shamanistic powers were able to take on the form of the creature who was their personal spirit helper. Composite figures showing this transformation are common.

Axangayuk's female head with bird (17) might also be interpreted as a spirit figure. The frightening aspect of the heavily tattooed face with its staring eyes and gap-toothed smile; the isolation of the head from any indication of a body creates uneasiness in the viewer. One could well imagine the bird to represent her spirit helper.

The use of incised decorations on ivory carvings dates back to prehistoric times. Post-contact trade items such as cribbage boards were commonly incised with designs or figures of men and animals blackened with lamp soot or ink.

Ipellie Osuitok, another renowned Cape Dorset artist, used this technique to embellish a muskox horn (49). His awareness of texture, volume and perspective in his illustrations is striking. Among the scenes of daily life is one of a carver at work; an interesting observation on the importance of this activity as part of everyday life in Cape Dorset. The long curve of the horn is finished at the tip as a bird's head. The rough surface of the base forms a pleasing contrast to the smooth form.

Another fine example of Osuitok's work is a muskox head with curved horns (114). Surprisingly enough, the muskox is a favourite subject of a number of South Baffin artists even though this animal never inhabited the area. Possibly the "exotic" nature of this beast, known through photographs and films, has inspired this interest. Certainly the bulky shape, the humped neck, the hanging shaggy coat provide a natural sculptural form.

Pudlo Pudlat, creator of the commissioned print "In Celebration" (4), has used muskoxen extensively as subject matter in his imaginative and often amusing drawings and acrylics. In an unpublished interview he has described the one time he had the opportunity to see a herd of muskoxen when the pilot of a small aeroplane on which he was a passenger circled low over a herd.

The subject of mother and child continues to be an important theme for Inuit artists but it was in Arctic Quebec during the period 1950-1960 that especially forceful examples of woman as a life-giving force were created. Akeaktashuk's carving of a mother carrying her child (29) expresses this maternal strength. The compact figure is powerfully forthright in her stance and facial expression. The ivory fish and scraper in her hands, the child riding in her amautik become symbols of her nurturing and procreative role.

The sculpture featured on the cover (1), carved by an unknown artist from Sugluk, is a powerfully evocative image of woman/mother. The clasped hands, the gently swaying stance, the fluid rounded shape conjure up an image of a woman rocking a baby. This idea is emphasized by the hollow formed by the bent arms. In fact, the baby being soothed is not visible, but indicated by the shape of the back pouch of the amautik where it is held. The grey lightly polished local stone of the body is minimally detailed, contrasting with the carefully modelled features of the inset flesh-toned face. The use of insets, usually ivory, for detail or sometimes for entire faces was common at this time. The piece is an extraordinary example of a sensitively conceived use of such an inset, both in the graduated skin tones of the stone and the wonderfully serene expression.

Man as hunter is another common theme. Most works show the man actively engaged in the hunt. Often he is holding a harpoon or other weapon, his stance expressive of his action — bending over a seal hole with locked knees, straining under the weight of his kill. In an unusual carving related to this theme, Markusi Anauta has given us an image of a sleeping man huddled under his parka, his boots used as a pillow

(65). It is easy to imagine the work representing "after the hunt". The details are minimal but used with telling effect — the open boot top and doubled hem of the folded parka frame the sleeping face; the thrown back hood opening and dangling sleeves of the parka emphasize the mood of total exhaustion. The compactness of form, the dark stone colour and the small size of the carving combine to generate an emotional response of protectiveness for the sleeper.

Humour is sometimes found in everyday events as in Davidialuk's carving of a seal caught in a net (168). The animal pokes its nose rather indignantly through the mesh and appears to wear one of the floats as a hat. Davidialuk, a major Povungnituk artist, often combined positive and negative spaces in his carvings. In this work the finely carved openwork net makes a subtle transition to incised lines as it crosses the form of the entangled seal.

Such playful portrayals of animals and birds are frequent. A delightful work by Peesee Oshuitoq (252) shows two bears dancing atop an ivory pedestal incised with pictures of an accordian player and a ring of dancing human figures.

Ivory, usually walrus tusk, was formerly a commonly used carving material. Included in the Guild collection is an exquisite example in which figures of animals, birds, men and sleds cover the tusk in an openwork pattern (282).

Ivory insets in stone carvings of the 1950s were common. In Inoucdjouac sometimes soap was used to fill in incised lines or dots to give the appearance of ivory. The collection includes a number of interesting examples of this technique (209, 14). In a carving of a mother owl with young (96) the eyes of the large owl are of inset ivory while those of the three owlets are of soap.

Ivory is used lavishly in a camp scene carved by Mark Tungilik of Repulse Bay about 1953 (48). In this fine example of folk art rectangular plates of ivory, attached to a block of wood with many copper nails, form a base for the scene; irregularly curved pieces of ivory are glued together in the shape of a snow house. The naive execution of these parts contrasts with sensitively fashioned figures such as the dog sheltering in the lee of the snow house, his nose tucked under his tail, or the delicately carved face and hair of the standing woman. The equipment of the camp is carefully detailed — the caribou antler handles of the sled are lashed on with sinew; the sealskin float is held high out of the reach of dogs, as are the drying skin boots; a snow shovel sticks out of the storage porch. The artist uses incised inked lines to emphasize details such as the individual snow blocks and the design on the woman's parka. A touch of colour is given in the pink tinted face of the baby.

Such scenes of daily life with figures glued or pegged to a base continue to be made but there is a growing tendency to integrate the base with the figures and to portray activity through the use of form and texture. In a major recent work, Lake Harbour artist Lucassie Ikkidluak has carved figures and base from one piece of stone (143). The base becomes an integral part of the scene, the land surface on which two hunters struggle to adjust a heavy pack. The work is technically daring with its interplay of positive and negative spaces. The fragility of the thinly-carved pack straps contrasts with the bulkily clothed figures; the areas of high polish are juxtaposed to the roughened base and textured hair and fur trousers of the figures. The entire composition is one of balance and strength.

In another contemporary work, a carved ivory tusk on a stone base in the shape of a seal (50), George Arluk of Baker Lake has integrated the two parts through the use of colour contrasts. Low relief carvings of men and animals on the tusk have inked-in details. The interplay of these dark markings on the ivory with white incisions on the dark stone of the base unify the work. Both parts are treated in a light-hearted, playful manner, further unifying the carving.

In both of these recent works the artists' awareness of the potential of their chosen medium and their successful completion of a planned and integrated whole is apparent. The approach is sculptural rather than descriptive. This is in marked contrast to earlier carvings in which the subject is of primary importance with sculptural considerations secondary. Indeed, the sense of form and balance so much a part of the carvings of the post-1950 era seems all the more marvellous for its instinctive nature.

Inuit carvers active today work within a tradition established at a time when daily life was totally integrated with nature: the land, the animals, the weather. Survival depended on an intimate knowledge of natural elements. Today the Inuit are part-time hunters based in permanent communities. Their carvings no longer reflect the former intimacy with natural forms but replace it with an awareness and aesthetic pleasure in depicting their cultural heritage through their art.

Helga Goetz
Inuit Art Specialist
Department of Indian
and Northern Affairs
Ottawa
1980

2. HELEN KALVAK 1901-
Holman Island
felt pen drawing 1969
58.0 x 42.5
354.

KALUAK

3. JESSIE OONARK 1906-
Baker Lake
ink drawing 1972
43.0 x 35.5
353.

Pudlo's lithograph, "In Celebration", was commissioned by the Canadian Guild of Crafts to commemorate the first exhibition of contemporary Eskimo Art held at the Guild on November 21, 1949.

The edition of 50 is printed on German etching paper using one stone and three aluminum plates with hand colouring in acrylics by the artist.

4. PUDLO PUDLAT 1916-
   Cape Dorset
   "In Celebration" 1979
   lithograph
   Cape Dorset catalogue 1980
   368.

5. KIAWAK ASHOONA 1933-
   (KIUGAK)
   Cape Dorset
   1960
   stone
   19.0 x 10.2 x 30.0
   157.

6. DAVIDIALUK ALASUA AMITTU 1910-1976
   Povungnituk
   batik 1972
   68.5 x 84.0
   341.

29

7. MARY SAVIADYUK 1897-c. 1971
   Sugluk
   1956
   stone
   15.0 x 8.5 x 18.0
   099.

8. UNIDENTIFIED ARTIST
   Inoucdjouac
   1954
   stone and ivory
   18.0 x 13.0 x 9.0
   134.

9. KIPANIK 1919-
   Lake Harbour
   1957
   stone
   10.0 x 10.0 x 7.5
   169.

10. UNIDENTIFIED ARTIST
Povungnituk
1957
stone
3.3 x 11.0 x 17.0
124.

11. SAROLIE WEETALUKTUK 1906-1962
    Inoucdjouac
    1958
    stone
    17.0 x 11.5 x 17.0
    066.

12. PUDLAT POOTOOGOOK 1919-
    Cape Dorset
    1955
    stone, ivory, wood and hair
    29.5 x 12.5 x 6.5
    049.

13

13. LEVI QUMALUK 1919-
    Povungnituk
    1949
    stone and soap inlay
    7.5 x 13.0 x 8.5
    360.

14

14. LEVI QUMALUK 1919-
    Povungnituk
    1949
    stone and soap inlay
    5.5 x 5.7 x 7.8
    213.

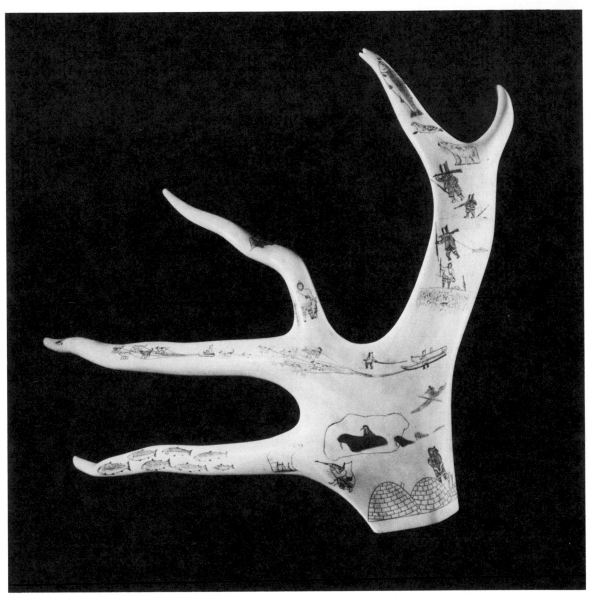

15. PAULASSIE POOTOOGOOK 1927-
Cape Dorset
1953
antler and stone inlay
39.0 x 51.0 x 3.6
298.

16. KIAWAK ASHOONA 1933-
    (KIUGAK)
    Cape Dorset
    1958
    stone
    13.0 x 15.5 x 6.0
    147.

17. AXANGAYUK SHAA 1937-
   (AQJANGAJUK)
   Cape Dorset
   1958
   stone
   14.0 x 24.0 x 12.0
   065.

18

19

18. LEVI AMIDLAK 1931-
    Inoucdjouac
    1952
    stone and ivory
    17.5 x 11.0 x 14.0
    164.

19. THOMASSIE ECHALUK 1935-
    Inoucdjouac
    1957
    stone
    17.5 x 9.0 x 10.0
    165.

20. ALLIE APPAQAQ 1915-
Belcher Islands
1964
stone
6.0 x 13.0 x 6.5
228.

21

22

21. SIMEONIE KINGALIK 1930-
    Inoucdjouac
    1954
    stone and ivory
    29.0 x 13.0 x 12.0
    160.

22. LOUIS OKSOKITOK 1926-
    Repulse Bay
    1966
    stone and ivory
    18.5 x 15.0 x 11.0
    217.

23. ANOTHER VIEW
of No. 22.

24. TOOTALUK
   Lake Harbour
   1957
   stone and ivory
   11.3 x 5.3 x 28.0
   305.

25. THOMASIE ANGOTIGIRK 1920-
    Povungnituk
    1957
    stone and ivory
    12.0 x 14.5 x 30.0
    182.

26. LEVI ECHALOOK 1918-
    Inoucdjouac
    1954
    stone and ivory
    16.5 x 19.0 x 7.0
    198.

27. TIMOTHY OTTOCHIE 1904-
Cape Dorset
1959
stone
15.5 x 9.8 x 7.0
069.

28. ABRAHAM ETUNGAT 1911-
Cape Dorset
1977
stone
29.0 x 22.0 x 12.0
359.

29. AKEEAKTASHUK 1898-1954
Inoucdjouac
1953
stone and ivory
11.0 x 6.0 x 7.5
075.

30. AKEEAKTASHUK 1898-1954
Inoucdjouac
1952
stone and ivory
11.5 x 5.0 x 9.0
084.

31. PAULOOSIE KANAJU 1937-
    Povungnituk
    1955
    stone, ivory and hide
    27.5 x 20.0 x 11.5
    063.

32

33

32. ELIJAH POOTOOGOOK 1943-
Cape Dorset
1957
stone
12.0 x 7.0 x 15.0
180.

33. UNIDENTIFIED ARTIST
Povungnituk
1961
stone
7.5 x 3.0 x 5.5
185.

34

34. TIKITUQ QINNUAYUAK 1908-
Cape Dorset
1953
stone and ivory
11.0 x 11.0 x 8.0
090.

35. UNIDENTIFIED ARTIST
Cape Dorset
1955
stone and glass beads
12.0 x 5.5 x 5.5
209.

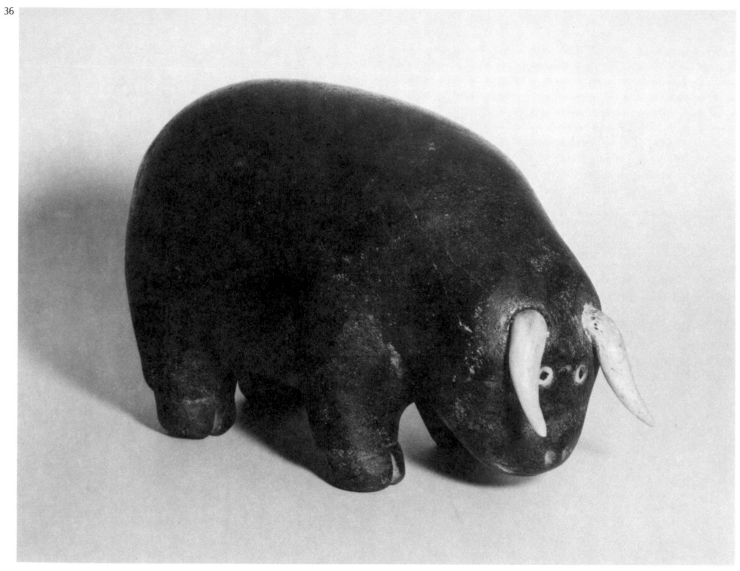

36. SAMUELLIE TUNNILLIE 1918-
Cape Dorset
1953
stone and ivory
13.5 x 8.5 x 19.0
247.

37

38

37. KAPIK KOLOLA 1926-
Lake Harbour
1962
stone
6.5 x 8.0 x 14.5
200.

38. LEVI AMIDLAK 1931-
Inoucdjouac
1953
stone and ivory
18.0 x 6.2 x 6.0
083.

39

40

41

39. UNIDENTIFIED ARTIST
Lake Harbour
1955
stone
3.5 x 5.5 x 12.6
248.

40. MANNUMI SHAQU 1917-
Cape Dorset
1965
stone
6.4 x 4.2 x 9.0
152.

41. SAGGIAK 1897-1980
Cape Dorset
1960
stone
9.0 x 5.2 x 4.5
153.

42. KADLOO KALLUK 1927-
    Arctic Bay
    1951
    stone and ivory
    4.6 x 3.4 x 1.5
    103.

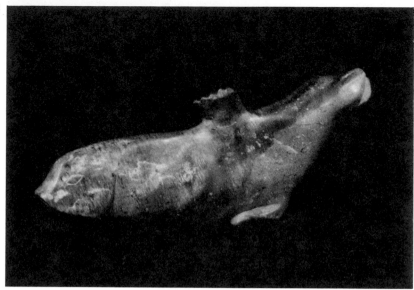

43. OTTOCHIE ASHOONA 1942-1970
    Cape Dorset
    1962
    stone
    19.0 x 31.0 x 7.2
    068.

44. AGGEAK PETAULASSIE 1922-
    Cape Dorset
    1955
    stone
    10.0 x 29.1 x 27.3
    203.

45. KANANGAQ ALOOLOO 1918-
(ELISAPEE)
Arctic Bay
1954
bone, ivory and stone
10.5 x 10.0 x 20.0
163.

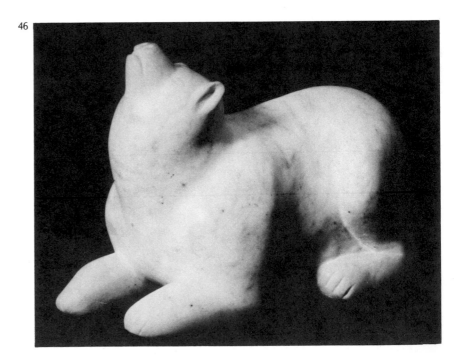

46. AGGEAK PETAULASSIE 1922-
Cape Dorset
1958
marble
10.5 x 6.8 x 13.5
161.

47. SAROLIE WEETALUKTUK 1906-1962
Inoucdjouac
1953
ivory
2.7 x 1.6 x 23.5
024.

48. MARK TUNGILIK 1913-
Repulse Bay
1953
ivory, stone, bone,
copper nails and wood
21.0 x 12.0 x 31.5
021.

49. IPELLIE OSUITOK
    (OSHOOWEETOOK "B")
    Cape Dorset
    1953
    muskox horn
    42.0 x 18.5 x 20.0
    302.

50. GEORGE ARLUK 1949-
    (ARLOOK)
    Baker Lake
    1980
    ivory and stone
    35.0 x 15.5 x 6.0
    366.

51

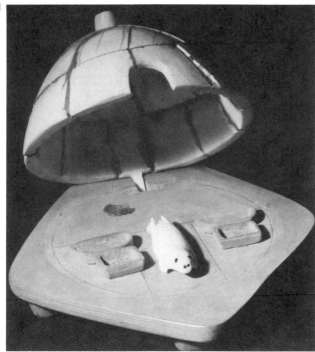

52

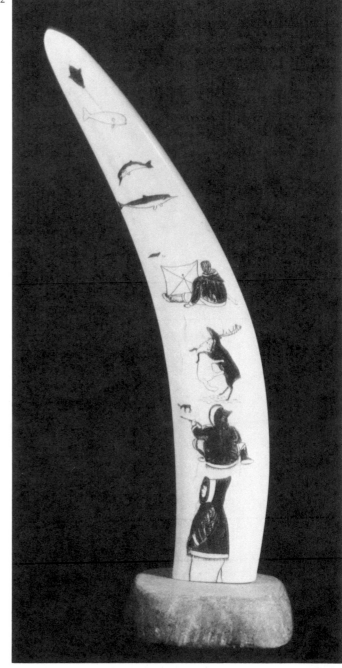

51. UNIDENTIFIED ARTIST
    Repulse Bay
    1952
    ivory and stone
    22.5 x 18.5 x 18.0
    029.

52. KIAWAK ASHOONA 1933-
    (KIUGAK)
    Cape Dorset
    1956
    ivory, stone and ink
    39.0 x 5.5 x 2.7
    019.

53

54

55

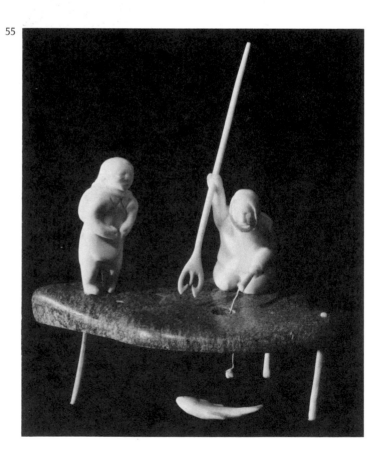

53. HENRY NAPARTUK 1932-
Great Whale River
1953
ivory and stone
5.5 x 3.3 x 9.0
016.

54. ELIJASSIAPIK 1912-1971
Inoucdjouac
1953
ivory and stone
4.0 x 2.4 x 28.0
033.

55. MADELEINE ISSERKUT 1928-
Repulse Bay
1968
ivory and stone
11.3 x 10.0 x 7.0
035.

56. UNIDENTIFIED ARTIST
Arctic Bay
1954
bone, ivory and stone
10.5 x 10.0 x 20.0
162.

57. AGLUK KOONAYOOK 1924-
Arctic Bay
1960
whale bone
9.0 x 9.0 x 15.5
204.

58. AKEEAKTASHUK 1898-1954
Inoucdjouac
1952
bone and ink
8.6 x 5.5 x 2.5
186.

59. JOHNNY ISSAJA PAPIGATOK 1923-
   Sugluk
   1965
   stone and ivory
   13.0 x 20.3 x 29.5
   119.

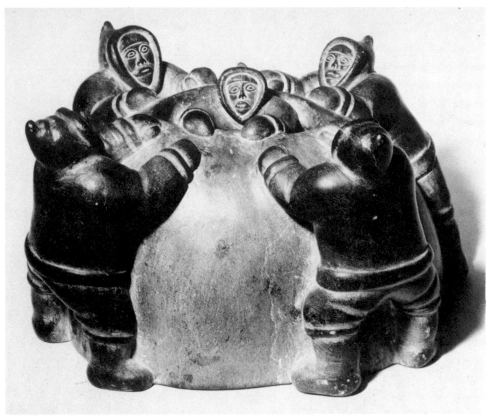

60. ABRAHAM POV 1927-
    Inoucdjouac
    1961
    stone
    14.5 x 24.5 x 24.5
    062.

61. LUKASI ANANAGI AMAMARTUA 1935-
    (AMAMATUK)
    Povungnituk
    1958
    stone
    29.0 x 12.2 x 9.3
    117.

62. AISA QUPIRUALU ALASUA 1916-
    (KOPERQUALOOK)
    Povungnituk
    1959
    stone and ivory
    23.2 x 29.0 x 18.5
    086.

63

63. UNIDENTIFIED ARTIST
Inoucdjouac
1953
stone and ivory
8.2 x 6.0 x 5.5
340.

64

64. KIPANIK 1919-
Lake Harbour
1957
stone, wood and ivory
5.7 x 4.8 x 15.5
096.

65. MAKUSI PANGUTU ANAUTA 1939-
(MARKOOSIE)
Povungnituk
1958
stone
6.5 x 11.5 x 5.0
107.

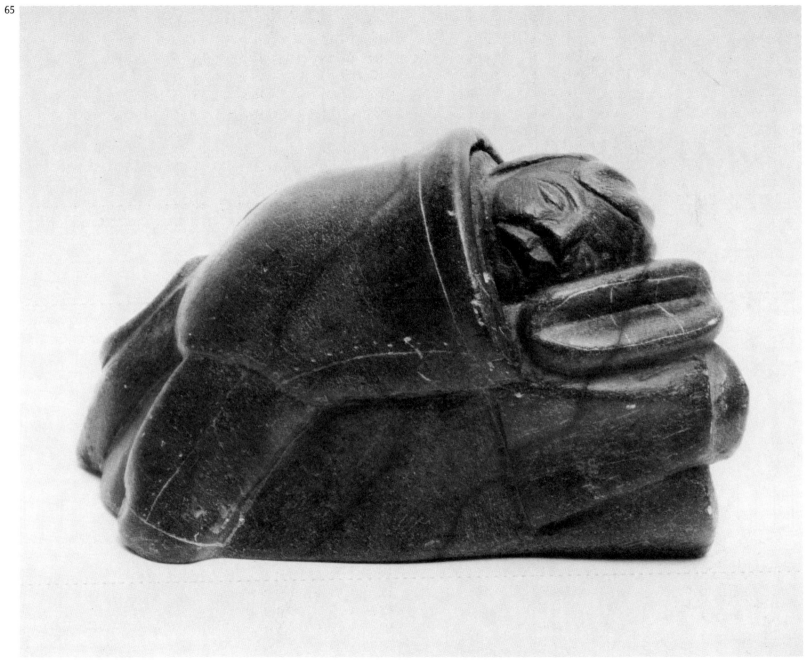

66. AISA QUMA IGAIJU 1915-
    (AISAPIK)
    Povungnituk
    1955
    stone
    19.0 x 21.0 x 20.3
    104.

67. PAUTA SAILA 1916-
    Cape Dorset
    1965
    stone
    7.0 x 7.2 x 16.3
    177.

68. AISA QUIRUALU ALASUA 1916-
    (KOPERQUALOOK)
    Povungnituk
    1957
    stone and hide
    18.5 x 16.0 x 10.5
    094.

69. UNIDENTIFIED ARTIST
   Great Whale River
   1955
   stone and ivory
   20.5 x 14.2 x 3.2
   098.

70. LEVI AMIDLAK 1931-
   Inoucdjouac
   1953
   stone and ivory
   13.1 x 5.5 x 5.0
   060.

71. AKEEAKTASHUK 1898-1954
Inoucdjouac
1954
stone and ivory
16.5 x 12.5 x 9.5
087.

72. DAVIDEE MANNUME 1919-1979
Cape Dorset
1953
stone and ivory
11.0 x 5.5 x 11.2
074.

73. PUDLAT POOTOOGOOK 1919-
Cape Dorset
1953
stone
12.0 x 7.1 x 10.2
070.

74. ABRAHAM POV 1927-
    Inoucdjouac
    1958
    stone
    17.1 x 12.3 x 9.0
    108.

75. KIAKSHUK 1886-1967
   Cape Dorset
   1958
   stone
   13.3 x 18.4 x 5.2
   208.

76. JACQUES KABLUITOK 1912-
   Repulse Bay
   1967
   stone and ivory
   12.5 x 10.0 x 7.5
   141.

77

77. MAKUSI QALINGO ANGUTIKIRQ 1899-
   Povungnituk
   1957
   stone
   8.0 x 13.5 x 34.0
   193.

78. SAROLIE WEETALUKTUK 1906-1962
Inoucdjouac
1953
ivory
4.5 x 2.5 x 34.0
026.

79. UNIDENTIFIED ARTIST
Arctic Bay
1960
whale bone and ivory
12.0 x 10.0 x 32.3
245.

80. EASTERN ARCTIC
   C. 1900
   ivory
   2.7 x 1.7 x 7.5
   050.

81. EMALOOTE EMAROEETAK 1934-
   Arctic Bay
   1960
   whale bone and ivory
   12.0 x 15.5 x 18.0
   140.

82. SALOMONIE POOTOOGOOK 1913-c. 1958
   Cape Dorset
   1953
   bone and ink
   15.5 x 4.0 x 3.0
   301.

80

81

82

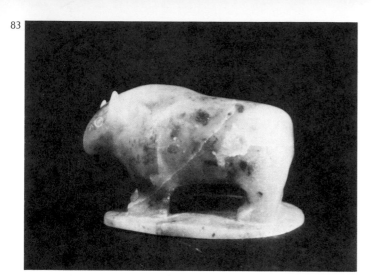

83. DOMINIQUE TUNGILIK 1920-
Gjoa Haven
1979
stone
6.0 x 6.5 x 7.5
363.

84. KIGUTIKARDJUK 1944-
Arctic Bay
1960
whale bone
17.0 x 17.5 x 13.0
244.

85. UNIDENTIFIED ARTIST
E9-1929
Sugluk
1959
stone and ivory
14.0 x 38.5 x 17.0
144.

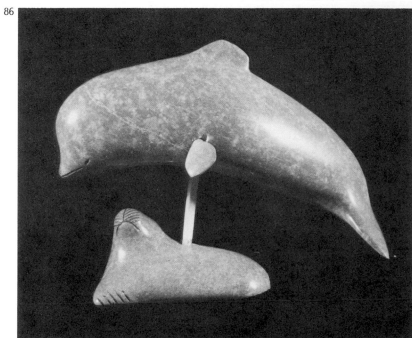

86. UNIDENTIFIED ARTIST
Lake Harbour
1957
stone and ivory
16.0 x 11.0 x 19.0
151.

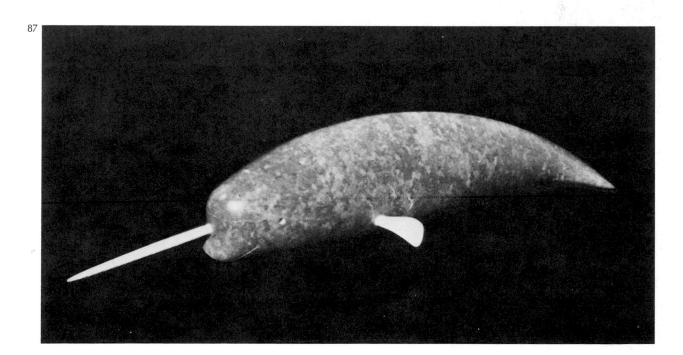

87. UNIDENTIFIED ARTIST
Lake Harbour
1958
stone and ivory
5.0 x 8.1 x 25.7
146.

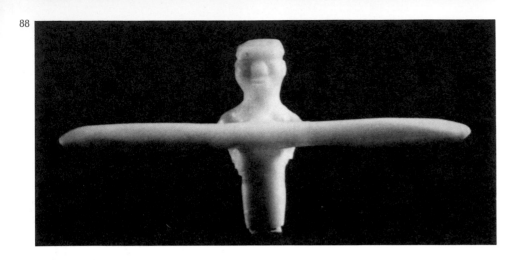

88. UNKNOWN AREA
   Kayak Man c. 1909
   ivory
   2.7 x 7.5 x 1.7
   052.

89. AGGEAK PETAULASSIE 1922-
   Cape Dorset
   1965
   stone
   5.5 x 7.5 x 14.5
   257.

90. UNIDENTIFIED ARTIST
   Sugluk
   1965
   stone
   12.0 x 10.5 x 10.0
   071.

91

91. UNIDENTIFIED ARTIST
Cape Dorset
1953
ivory and stone
6.0 x 3.0 x 5.5
030.

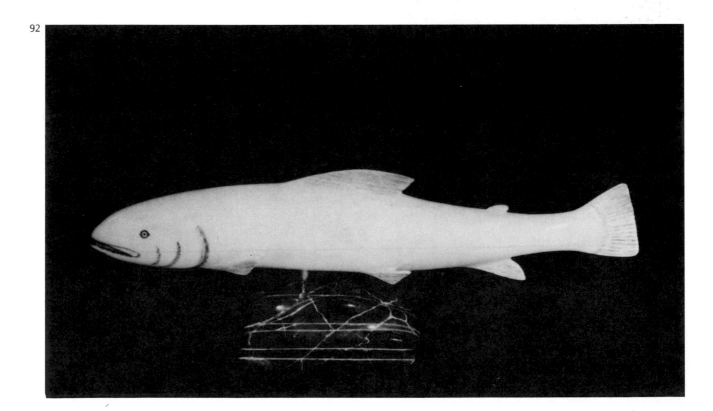

92

92. SHEOYUQ OQUTAQ 1920-
(SHEEOKJUKE)
Cape Dorset
1957
ivory, stone and ink
7.5 x 3.0 x 18.0
027.

93. SAKKEASSIE RAGEE 1924-
   Cape Dorset
   1951
   stone and soap inlay
   9.2 x 4.5 x 5.0
   166.

94. ADAMIE PAPYARLUK 1919-
   Great Whale River
   1953
   stone
   single bird: 9.2 x 1.6 x 8.0
   236.

95. SAROLIE WEETALUKTUK 1906-1962
   Inoucdjouac
   1953
   stone and ivory
   11.0 x 5.2 x 11.3
   250.

96. LEVI AMIDLAK 1931-
    Inoucdjouac
    1954
    stone, ivory and soap inlay
    15.0 x 16.3 x 5.2
    197.

97

98

97. SIMON KASUDLUAK 1925-
    (SIMON POV)
    Inoucdjouac
    1956
    stone
    9.0 x 3.5 x 12.2
    188.

98. LEVI AMIDLAK 1931-
    Inoucdjouac
    1954
    stone
    5.6 x 5.4 x 12.8
    174.

99. UNIDENTIFIED ARTIST
    Inoucdjouac
    1954
    stone and ivory
    11.5 x 9.0 x 21.2
    253.

99

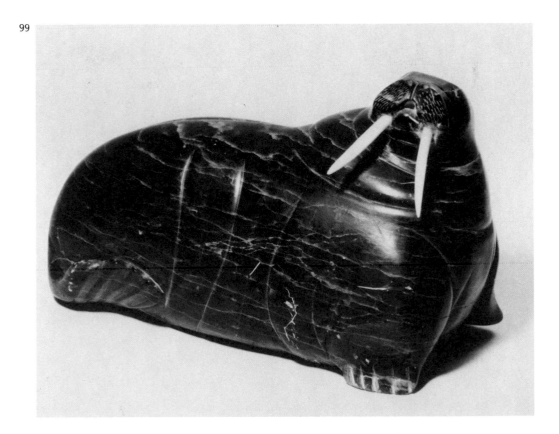

100. SAIMOUTIK deceased
Povungnituk
1953
stone and ivory
7.2 x 6.1 x 4.5
081.

101. SAIMOUTIK deceased
Povungnituk
1953
stone and soap inlay
17.0 x 8.2 x 5.5
077.

102. UNIDENTIFIED ARTIST
Inoucdjouac
1954
stone and ivory
29.0 x 29.2 x 7.5
299.

103

104

105

103. ABRAHAM NASTAPOKA 1900-
Inoucdjouac
1962
stone and ivory
9.5 x 3.8 x 6.1
073

104. ELIASSIEPIK 1913-1960
Povungnituk
1953
stone and ivory
7.5 x 16.8 x 16.0
310.

105. PAULUSI SIVUAK ALASUA 1930-
Povungnituk
1968
stone
14.5 x 11.5 x 14.0
357.

106. KIAWAK ASHOONA 1933-
(KIUGAK)
Cape Dorset
1962
stone
26.0 x 6.5 x 33.0
158.

108. TIMOTHY OTTOCHIE 1904-
    Cape Dorset
    1953
    stone (calcite) and ink
    9.2 x 7.3 x 7.9
    215.

107. DAVIDEE PIUNGITUQ 1930-
    (PEEONGEETOOK)
    Clyde River
    1974
    whale bone
    23.0 x 27.2 x 13.1
    138.

110

109. QAQAQ ASHOONA 1938-
    (KAKA)
    Cape Dorset
    1953
    stone
    10.0 x 5.5 x 8.0
    241.

110. UNIDENTIFIED ARTIST
    Repulse Bay
    1961
    whale bone
    17.5 x 6.0 x 5.5
    143.

111. DONAT ANAWAK 1920-
Repulse Bay
1953
stone and bone
4.5 x 4.5 x 19.0
125.

112. ANGATUK NASSAK 1931-
Payne Bay
1960
stone
9.1 x 4.5 x 5.0
080.

113. MARKUSI PAPIGATOK 1906-1971
Sugluk
1955
stone and ivory
26.5 x 17.0 x 23.0
172.

114

115

114. IPELLIE OSUITOK 1923-
    (OSHOOWEETOOK "B")
    Cape Dorset
    1955
    stone and muskox horn
    13.0 x 7.5 x 13.0
    064.

115. SHUVIGAR EELEE 1904-
    (SHOOVEEGAR)
    Cape Dorset
    1953
    stone and ivory
    10.5 x 7.5 x 4.0
    079.

116. PAULASSIE POOTOOGOOK 1927-
Cape Dorset
1968
stone
12.0 x 7.6 x 18.0
159.

117. ALAKU WEETALUKTUK deceased
     Ungava Region
     before 1938
     ivory
     3.0 x 2.5 x 31.5
     020.

118. MADELEINE ISSERKUT 1928-
     Repulse Bay
     1968
     ivory
     5.0 x 7.0 x 5.5
     367.

119

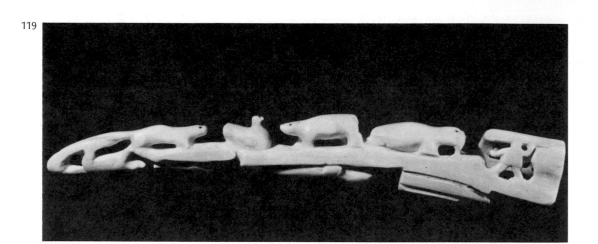

119. SAROLIE WEETALUKTUK 1906-1962
Inoucdjouac
1953
ivory
22.0 x 4.0 x 2.7
051.

120

120. MARK TUNGILIK 1913-
Repulse Bay
1953
ivory, wood, stone, metal,
sealskin, sinew and hide
sled: 2.0 x 5.0 x 15.5
028.

121

121. KUPPAPIK RAGEE 1931-
     (KOPAPIK)
     Cape Dorset
     1960
     stone
     13.0 x 8.2 x 30.0
     122.

122

122. KUPPAPIK RAGEE 1931-
     (KOPAPIK)
     Cape Dorset
     1957
     stone and sinew
     10.0 x 14.0 x 26.0
     120.

123

123. UNIDENTIFIED ARTIST
Povungnituk
1958
stone
9.0 x 4.5 x 11.0
106.

124

124. TIMOTHY KUTCHAKA 1924-
Inoucdjouac
1955
stone
15.0 x 10.0 x 25.0
100.

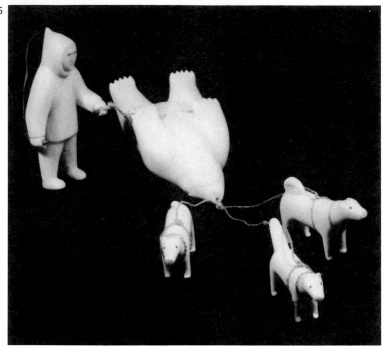

125

126

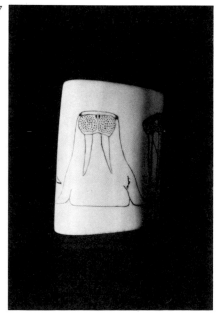

127

125. MARK TUNGILIK 1913-
Repulse Bay
1953
ivory, sinew and hide
8.0 x 11.0 x 21.0
013.

126. LUCY ANGALAKTE NAPSALAK 1931-
Repulse Bay
1961
bone, ivory and baleen
13.0 x 9.0 x 13.2
199.

127. UNIDENTIFIED ARTIST
Cape Dorset
1956
ivory and ink
6.0 x 4.0 x 3.5
018.

128. KIAWAK ASHOONA 1933-
(KIUGAK)
Cape Dorset
1958
stone
24.0 x 27.3 x 16.2
202.

129. UNIDENTIFIED ARTIST
Repulse Bay
1953
stone and wood
6.5 x 10.7 x 6.0
116.

130. SAMSON KINGALIK 1937-
Inoucdjouac
1960
stone
7.5 x 7.3 x 16.0
176.

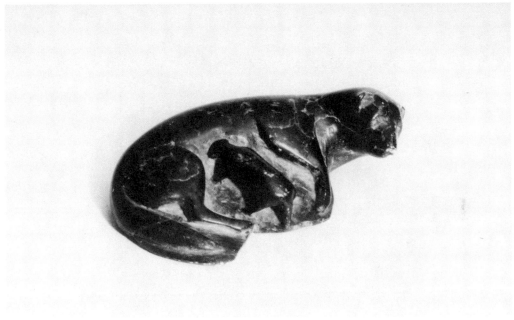

131. AISA QUPIRUALU ALASUA 1916-
(KOPERQUALOOK)
Povungnituk
1954
stone
3.0 x 5.5 x 10.2
189.

132. SIMON KASUDLUAK 1925-
(SIMON POV)
Inoucdjouac
1960
stone
9.0 x 6.2 x 17.0
184.

133. LUCASSIE KUMARLUK 1921-
    Inoucdjouac
    1955
    stone and ivory
    20.0 x 16.0 x 16.0
    061.

134

135

136

134. UNIDENTIFIED ARTIST
Inoucdjouac
1955
stone and ivory
16.0 x 15.0 x 20.0
095.

135. QINUAJUA
(KINGWAK)
Povungnituk
1952
stone, ivory and hide
5.5 x 5.0 x 13.0
059.

136. PETER QUMALUK deceased
Inoucdjouac
1957
stone and ivory
14.5 x 17.0 x 12.0
252.

137. SAJUILI AMITTU 1932-
    (SAYOLIE ARPATUK)
    Povungnituk
    1958
    stone
    6.2 x 16.0 x 9.0
    114.

138. PAULOSIE WEETALUKTUK 1938-
    Inoucdjouac
    1958
    stone and hide
    20.0 x 10.5 x 9.0
    110.

139. SIMON KASUDLUAK 1925-
    (SIMON POV)
    Inoucdjouac
    1957
    stone and ivory
    8.0 x 5.0 x 7.0
    206.

140. AISA QUMA IGAIJU 1915-
     (AISAPIK)
     Povungnituk
     1955
     stone
     26.5 x 18.0 x 8.5
     128.

141. PAULOSIE QUANANAK 1899-1963
Povungnituk
1955
stone and ivory
9.5 x 6.5 x 6.0
078.

142. ISA SMILER 1921-
Inoucdjouac
1957
stone
7.6 x 10.5 x 13.0
255.

143. LUCASSIE IKKIDLUAK 1949-
Lake Harbour
1977
stone
30.0 x 34.0 x 39.0
356.

144. IRENE KATAQ 1914-1971
Repulse Bay
1961
whale bone
5.2 x 6.1 x 4.0
142.

145. UNIDENTIFIED ARTIST
Repulse Bay
1966
ivory and bone
2.8 x 4.8 x 14.0
039.

146. KIAKSHUK 1886-1967
Cape Dorset
1958
stone (calcite) and ink
7.0 x 7.0 x 7.0
242.

147

147. UNIDENTIFIED ARTIST
Repulse Bay
1964
ivory and stone
5.6 x 2.2 x 4.5
036.

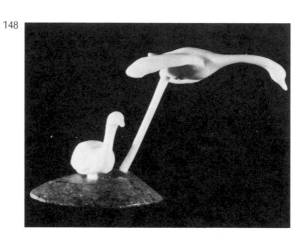

148

148. IRENE KATAQ 1914-1971
Repulse Bay
1968
ivory and stone
4.5 x 3.5 x 5.0
041.

149

149. UNIDENTIFIED ARTIST
Lake Harbour
1955
stone
10.0 x 28.2 x 1.2
246.

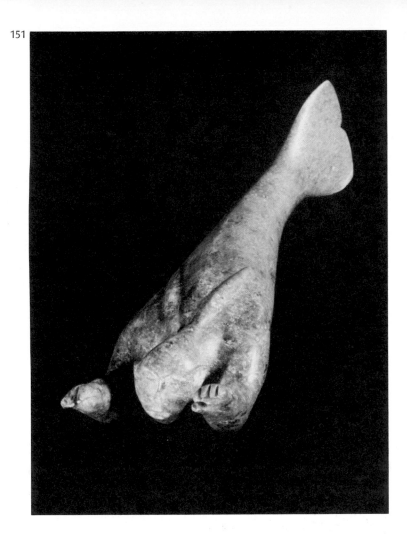

150. SAGGIAK 1897-1980
Cape Dorset
1960
stone
5.5 x 13.0 x 24.5
148.

151. SAGGIAK 1897-1980
Cape Dorset
1960
stone
5.6 x 7.0 x 27.5
149.

152. 2 views
KIAWAK ASHOONA 1933-
(KIUGAK)
Cape Dorset
1954
stone
25.0 x 15.0 x 14.5
118.

153. UNIDENTIFIED ARTIST
    Cape Dorset
    1961
    stone
    22.0 x 14.5 x 30.0
    155.

154

155

156

154. THOMASIE ANGUTIGIRK 1920-
Sugluk
1955
stone
21.5 x 15.0 x 10.0
131.

155. SIMEONIE OPIK 1928-
Belcher Islands
1973
stone and ivory
13.0 x 17.4 x 34.2
312.

156. UNIDENTIFIED ARTIST
Povungnituk
1955
stone and ivory
11.0 x 21.5 x 20.5
130.

157. ABRAHAM ETUNGAT 1911-
Cape Dorset
1977
stone
30.0 x 13.2 x 19.3
358.

159. UNIDENTIFIED ARTIST
Inoucdjouac
1953
stone and bone
5.0 x 2.0 x 7.5
187.

158. KONAK c. 1937-
Inoucdjouac
1951
stone and ink
6.5 x 3.5 x 6.5
137.

160. JOANASSIE RAGEE 1935-
Cape Dorset
1953
stone
9.5 x 7.0 x 15.0
240.

161. UNIDENTIFIED ARTIST
Cape Dorset
1955
stone, ivory and fish bone
18.5 x 4.0 x 3.5
150.

162

163

164

162. LUCASSIE NOWYA 1924-
Great Whale River
1959
stone
7.0 x 4.5 x 16.3
233.

163. MOSES APPAQAQ 1926-
Belcher Islands
1964
stone
4.0 x 2.2 x 8.1
235.

164. TIMOTHY KUTCHAKA 1924-
Inoucdjouac
1957
stone
12.5 x 6.5 x 19.0
212.

165. QAQAQ ASHOONA 1928-
(KAKA)
Cape Dorset
1955
stone
25.2 x 14.0 x 14.5
115.

166. Attributed to:
LEVI AMIDLAK 1931-
Povungnituk
1951
stone and sinew
4.7 x 4.0 x 2.2
089.

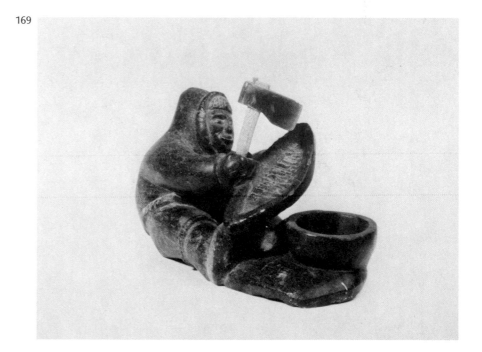

167. DAVIDIALUK ALASUA AMITTU 1910-1976
Povungnituk
1958
stone
3.5 x 7.5 x 8.0
192.

168. DAVIDIALUK ALASUA AMITTU 1910-1976
Povungnituk
1958
stone
8.0 x 5.5 x 11.5
196.

169. DAVIDIALUK ALASUA AMITTU 1910-1976
Povungnituk
1958
stone and wood
10.0 x 7.5 x 15.0
092.

170. PETER PITSEOLAK 1905-1973
Cape Dorset
1962
stone
20.0 x 24.3 x 11.2
239.

171. ETOSACK SAMSACK 1916-
Inoucdjouac
1953
stone and ivory
12.3 x 6.0 x 7.2
207.

172. PETER SAVIADJUK 1930-
     Lake Harbour
     1958
     stone
     10.0 x 5.0 x 3.5
     173.

173. UNIDENTIFIED ARTIST
Povungnituk
1955
stone and ivory
10.0 x 16.2 x 20.5
085.

174

175

176

174. ALLIE APPAQAQ 1915-
Belcher Islands
1964
stone
7.0 x 13.5 x 12.0
227.

175. JOHANASSIE TOOKALUK 1912-
Belcher Islands
1964
stone
7.5 x 5.5 x 7.5
230.

176. UNIDENTIFIED ARTIST
Povungnituk
1954
stone and ivory
12.0 x 15.5 x 24.0
254.

177

178

177. JOSIE PAMIUTU PAPIALUK 1918-
(JOSIE PAPPY)
Povungnituk
1965
stone
10.0 x 7.2 x 2.5
113.

178. TUKIKIKALU 1945-
Cape Dorset
1953
stone
5.5 x 5.0 x 14.5
183.

179

179. KALAI ADLA 1927-
(KLY)
Cape Dorset
1965
stone
9.0 x 3.5 x 15.0
175.

180. ELI ELIJASSIAPIK 1936-
Inoucdjouac
1957
stone
9.2 x 7.2 x 17.0
194.

181. SIMEONIE WEETALUKTUK 1921-
Inoucdjouac
1962
stone
12.0 x 8.2 x 12.5
112.

182

183

184

182. GEORGE KAMIDLAK 1941-
Coppermine
1971
stone
6.0 x 3.2 x 15.3
170.

183. SAKKEASSIE RAGEE 1924-
Cape Dorset
1962
stone
16.2 x 8.0 x 18.0
179.

184. TUDLIK 1890-1960
Cape Dorset
1953
stone
7.5 x 3.5 x 8.5
171.

185. SHARKY NUNA 1918-1979
Cape Dorset
1978
stone
10.0 x 17.0 x 2.5
364.

186. UNIDENTIFIED ARTIST
Inoucdjouac
1953
stone
6.5 x 4.5 x 14.0
167.

187. MUNGITOK 1940-
Cape Dorset
"Canada Geese"
stonecut No. 34/1959
Cape Dorset catalogue
348.

ESKIMO ART: A SOCIAL REALITY

The development of Eskimo art is closely allied with the cooperative movement in Arctic Canada and neither can be understood without an examination of their linkages in the past and their role in Inuit development. Both are culturally grounded, incorporating values from a lifestyle which developed almost completely undisturbed over thousands of years. At the same time, they have been important modernizing influences, responsible for initiating economic development and consequent social change among Inuit. Although there is inherent strain and sometimes outright contradiction, in pursuing a role as mediator between a traditional and a modern lifestyle, the co-op and the arts programmes have managed to bring Inuit into a business relation with the rest of the country without — and this is most important — causing a major social disruption.

My purpose here is to place the cooperatives and their art programmes in a development continuum, demonstrating that while they have been responsible for linking Inuit to the modern world economy, they have also allowed for the transmission of values generated in a former lifestyle.

Left to develop on their own, Inuit had thousands of years to hone the skills which enabled them to cope with a grudging environment. They made, literally, the best of their situation, perfecting an efficient technology from the most meagre of resources. Their lifestyle was geared to survival of the most basic sort: to eat and to be protected from the elements. The main resource was the wild animal and Inuit learned to use every bone and fibre of those they captured. The flesh provided food; the skins clothing. Bone was used for sled runners and needles as well as for tent and kayak frames which were then re-covered with skin. Stone was carved into pots and lamps to be fuelled by blubber. Bone, stone and ivory were used to fashion tools, weapons, amulets and toys. Even the wind-packed snow was used. In typically ingenious fashion, it was carved into building blocks for the structurally remarkable igloo.

For obvious reasons, the hunt was the activity around which all life was ordered. The availability of game dictated what clothing Inuit wore, what food they ate, where they lived, or indeed, whether they lived. The hunt was also the focus of their religion which consisted of rituals and taboos governing the relationship of man with the beasts. The wild creatures must be treated with respect; for Inuit did not consider themselves to be masters of nature but rather, lived in a state of constant fear lest they offend those upon whom they depended for survival.

In an environment which offered few options, only the skillful and/or lucky survived for long. Harsh as it may sound, the law of the wild prevailed, weeding out the incompetent and frail who were a hindrance to themselves and to everybody else. There was no welfare, no medical help, no unemployment insurance to take up the slack for the weak or unlucky. Those who couldn't pull their own weight were, mercifully enough, left behind when the group moved on in its everlasting pursuit for food. Such was the fate of those too old to help even themselves and of female babies when they would have been a burden rather than a help to the group. It was, in unadorned language, a do or die situation and self-sufficiency was the chief adaptive trait.

The necessity of chasing after their food meant that Inuit were always on the move. They travelled in small family groups which were really, the unit of survival. If a family could not provide for itself, it perished. It was as simple as that. The male hunted and the female converted the fruits of his labour to clothing. Children aided in these tasks according to their age and sex. The skills of male and female were interdependent and the survival of the group depended very much on the abilities each brought to necessary tasks. Chance also played a role but this was something which no man could control. One was careful not to offend the animal spirits, and still, things might not go well. In this case, the only practical attitude was acceptance. In such a manner did the harmony of their universe continue undisturbed.

Everything Inuit did was directed towards the maintenance of harmony. Ownership, the cause of strife elsewhere in the world, was not a viable concept among Eskimos who considered that what existed, whether it be food or land, was there to be used by all. They had the good sense to perceive, that while competition is wasteful, concerted effort conserves energy and maximizes returns. Practicality prevailed in all matters and for the most part, the people lived together without wars.

Operating at a simple and naturally democratic level of social organization, they also lived without kings and formal laws. Prior to settling permanently in towns, Inuit had hunted from camps situated within a hundred mile radius of the Hudson's Bay Company trading posts. Because of the difficulty of hunting food, the groups were small, seldom more than ten related families although they occasionally included a few non-relatives. These camp groups were not "tribes", nor were there "chiefs" although the senior male member of the group was naturally deferred to as the decision-maker. These informal camp "bosses" assumed authority in a non-authoritarian way, for organizing their relatives in the daily challenge of finding food.

Although Inuit had, by the beginning of this century, developed a taste for the white man's goods, particularly guns and ammunition, they managed to perpetuate their more or less self-sufficient lifestyle for several decades more, due no doubt, to their isolation in one of the world's most uninviting environments.

European explorers had been in the Canadian Arctic as early as the sixteenth century but there was little sustained contact with the outside world until the early 1900's. Although the first trading post had been established at Richmond Gulf in 1749, it was not until the early twentieth century that trading posts, in some cases swelled by a mission and an RCMP detachment, became active centres, capable of exerting an organizing influence upon Inuit lifestyle. It was around this time that the Canadian government began to show an interest in its Arctic regions. For a long while its interest focussed on the potential of the land rather than the people and it was not until after the second world war that social programmes were put into place and towns were born.

Inuit gradually left their camps and moved into these towns, mainly in order to be near medical help and schools. In Arctic Quebec the abandonment of camp life was accelerated by TB surveys conducted in 1955-56. In some cases, as much as one third of the camp population was evacuated to southern sanitoria where they stayed for one or more years. Some, of course, never returned. Almost every family had to send members away to hospital and those left behind gradually drifted into the communities, taking up a new lifestyle which depended heavily upon outside support and which plunged them headlong into a greatly accelerated rate of acculturation.

Early contact had been on a one to one basis. The information received from the lone trader or visiting missionary, although biased, occurred at a speed which did not overwhelm the Eskimo who was used to having time to think. Besides, prior to the establishment of villages, Inuit more or less controlled contact with foreigners, going in to trade at the post only occasionally. How bewildering it must have been for them to move from a situation where everyone and everything that mattered was known, to a situation where unrelated people lived closely together but pursued individual goals. When they moved into towns, contact could no longer be governed by Inuit but became a feature of daily life, often beyond their comprehension and control. Although they were the numerical majority, Inuit townsmen were an effective minority as the structure of town life was organized by the itinerant white population — teachers, administrators, police, traders, nurses and missionaries.

The stress of acculturation is evident in spite of the fact that Inuit, accommodating by nature, have offered little resistance. It is the accelerated rate of change, rather than change per se, which has posed most problems for them. A culture which had, in thousands of years, not progressed beyond providing the necessities of life — food, clothing, housing, transportation — was abruptly exposed to a random dose of twentieth century fringe benefits. The "Eskimo Way" when confronted with an alteration in circumstance, was to talk about it until all agreed. Only when unanimous agreement had been reached would action be taken. Too much happened too fast and before they could think, let alone decide about it, Inuit were caught up in a lifestyle totally outside their experience.

The first Eskimo townsmen, with memories of having lived off the land, only dimly appreciated the consequences of losing their old skills and independence. It wasn't until the 70's, however, when the first generation of town born and bred Inuit were in their twenties, that the ramifications of change began to be appreciated and efforts mounted to counter the movement towards wholesale adoption of a foreign lifestyle. Because they had never known another life, the young were more at home in the white world than their fathers had been. They provided at one and the same time, both the impetus and the instrument to redress the balance. The older generation saw the young as casualties of acculturation but it was because of their facility in dealing with white institutions that the younger generation both needed and were able to champion Eskimo culture and take up the cause of Inuit self-determination. Eskimo politics was born in the 70's.

Inuit Tapirisat of Canada (ITC), a national political association, was formed in 1970 by Inuit students living in southern Canada. Their first official act was to announce that they preferred to be called "Inuit" (their own name for themselves) rather than "Eskimo", the name given them by the Indians and by which they were known all over the world. The Northern Quebec Inuit Association (NQIA) was formed soon after and in 1976 they signed the first treaty between the government and Canadian Inuit.

Political and cultural organizations proliferated across the Arctic in the next few years, often with overlapping membership as well as aims because of the small population they served. The global aim of all these ethnic associations is to ensure that Inuit have some say in what happens to them. Now that Inuit have a voice, they also have direct access to the top political echelon and are negotiating rights for Inuit in a reformed Canadian constitution. They are also able to form international alliances. At the Inuit Circumpolar Conference held in Greenland this year, they agreed with Eskimos from all over the world, that it was in their best interests to retain control over their land and its resources. Inuit in the Northwest Territories, who have not yet concluded an Agreement with the Canadian Government have already announced their intention of negotiating the creation of a new ethnic political territory to be called "Nunavut".

Apart from organized attempts to determine their future, informal movements aimed at cultural preservation have been gaining ground in the last decade. The now widespread "back to the land" movement got underway in the 70's and many villages become ghost towns in summer when their Inuit populations move out to the land to pursue, at least seasonally, an alternative lifestyle. Some talk about, and a few have tried, a permanent move back but this, for environmental reasons, has not proved feasible. Other aspects of the cultural revival movement are the ongoing efforts to perpetuate the Eskimo language and to re-learn hunting and handicraft techniques which became increasingly irrelevant as the culture underwent an externally generated transformation.

The material changes are relatively easy to document. Although it has been to the peril of their own material culture, Inuit easily mastered twentieth century technology. Guns replaced harpoons and it wasn't long before boats with motors had largely taken the place of kayaks and snowmobiles had replaced dog teams. Metal needles and woven cloth replaced bone needles and animal pelts. Leaving their skin tents and igloos, people moved into wooden houses and preserved food released them from dependence upon country food.

The certain consequence of having a ready supply of goods and an alternative means of living is the loss of formerly necessary abilities. Predictably enough, Inuit have forgotten many of the skills which were passed in an apprentice tradition, through generations of their ancestors. Predictably too, the traits they had developed to enable them to live in peace in their formidable environment have not always proven useful in coping with a foreign lifestyle.

One of the first effects of town living was the deterioration of formerly self-reliant people into dependent people.[1] Formerly constrained to procure the things they needed through the application of their own abilities, they became dependent upon a foreign structure for a steady supply of material goods. It was soon obvious that Inuit could not sustain village life without the presence of whites who ran all the institutions in the north and had direct lines to outside support systems. More discomposing than their dependence upon manufactured goods and imported services, was their increasing reference to the priorities of outsiders to pattern daily life. In the past, faced with the necessity of performing certain key tasks at a seasonally determined time, the Eskimo made his own decisions. There was a time for catching caribou and a time for making clothes. In town however, the coordination of thought and effort formerly required to live was no longer pertinent. The change from camp to town life had disrupted, forever it seemed, the natural rhythm of a life perfected through centuries of trial and error learning.

It seemed as if Inuit were destined for wholesale assimilation into the western world. Many were even measuring their "progress" in terms of how much like the white man they were becoming. Although sending their children to school disrupted their lives and imperiled their language, they did it because they believed education to be the key to sharing in the white man's awesome power and technology.

Although assimilation was the effect, if not the intent of most northern programmes, there was a countervailing force in the cooperative movement which began in the late 50's and soon spread to virtually every village across the Arctic. Although it recognized the need for Inuit to "catch up" with the twentieth century, the cooperative operated on the premise that it was possible to update Eskimo thinking without violating cultural values. The traditional sharing of the proceeds of the hunt was no longer practical in communities of several hundred people, but the co-op, by offering it for sale at low prices, ensured that it continued to be available to the community, albeit on more practical terms and more in tune with the modern business world.

Cultural preservation has always been a prime motivating force in the Eskimo cooperative movement. Before the 70's, the co-op was the only organized voice Inuit had. Until very recently, the cooperative functioned as an "underground government",[2] pushing the self-determination issue long before it was taken up by Inuit Tapirisat and the regional political bodies.[3] In fact, many of the new Associations are manned by co-op "graduates" who took with them the idea that Inuit can be, as they once were, self-sufficient.

It is unlikely that the political potential of co-ops was realized by its early promoters, many of them federal government employees. They were considered, simply, as being the best opportunity for newly urbanized Inuit to prosper economically. The co-op succeeded in winning Inuit allegiance, not because of its economic potential but because of its cultural compatibility. Based on the idea of pooling resources, it was seen as a logical evolution from the old camp life when no one was really boss and everyone shared in decisions and profits. Non-government whites, notably the Roman Catholic missionaries, became fervent promoters of the co-op philosophy, assuring the northern people that it was a way for them to regain some of their lost independence, a compelling argument for many Inuit who were just beginning to realize and regret its loss.[4] They were attracted by the argument that co-ops would allow them to progress as Inuit, rather than, as other programmes seemed designed to do, turn them into white men.

The co-op, it appeared, was the best available vehicle for reconciling Inuit to the exigencies of modern economic life while at the same time, safeguarding those features of traditional life which had always stood them in good stead — communal ownership, democratic decision-making, cooperative work efforts and a self-sufficient lifestyle. Significantly, the co-op has become known as the "Guardian of the Old Way" although this is used somewhat disparagingly by those who applaud the growing western lifestyle of Inuit and deplore their adherence to the past. As the Inuk leader of NQIA puts it, *Do they want us to become antiques?*[5] It is Inuit, now, who are promoting assimilation.

The arts and crafts programmes and the cooperative movement have been so closely linked from the beginning, that it is meaningless to consider them separately. Paulosie Kasadluak from Inoucdjouac expressed this rather nicely in "Things Made by Inuit", published by la Fédération des Coopératives du Nouveau-Québec this year: *"Although it (carving) enables the individual to earn a living for himself, it is not an individual activity. Inuit, as always, work through cooperation. Carvings and crafts have formed the foundation upon which our cooperatives (the first Eskimo businesses) were built and grew. In this way, the work of carving has strengthened and perpetuated the culture of the Inuit."*

Although the first carvings had been offered for sale in the south in 1949,[6] more than ten years before the incorporation of any Eskimo co-op, it was the cooperatives who organized the large-scale distribution of arts and crafts as well as assuming some of the developmental functions formerly exercised by the federal government.[7] Many, if not most of the people involved in the programme at that time considered Eskimo carving to be a craft, an effective way to lighten the welfare load. The fledgling co-ops were smart enough to realize its potential and succeeded in the two-fold task of encouraging the development of art along with the craft, and making the whole programme an economic success.

In some cases, Cape Dorset and Povungnituk, a carving programme, cooperative in nature, was underway before being formally incorporated into a Cooperative Association. In other cases, carving programmes were deliberately introduced as the economic base of newly incorporated Cooperatives. Although Arctic co-ops have diversified into a range of other producer/consumer activities — retail stores, oil delivery, commercial fishing, tourist camps, hotels — arts and crafts programmes continue to provide the economic underpinnings of the movement and this year will generate something like five million dollars in personal income for Inuit.

Apart from being mutually supportive in an economic sense, the cooperatives and the carving programmes share an ideology. The cooperative is viewed as an up-date on the old way of life while carving is merely a new use for an old skill. Because of their deep roots in Inuit history, both are valued as a way of participating in the twentieth century wage economy[8] without sacrificing one's "Eskimoness". As Peter Aullaluk from Ivujivik said in 1980: *"We will never go back to our traditional way of life, but our claim to be Inuit we seem to have forgotten ... using cooperatives, we are encouraged to continue as Inuit".*[9]

The co-op's role as mediator between the old and the new ways of life necessitates an often fine balancing of cultural and business prerogatives. The co-op allows for the transmission of culturally grounded values but it has also had to acknowledge the necessity of introducing new concepts and structures into Eskimo life. The carving and crafts programme meant that for the first time in his role as producer, a man was freed from eternal dependence upon luck and had control over the means to secure a reasonably steady supply of food.[10] As important, was the fact that he was able to do this without major disruption to his social life since carvers and craftsmen are able, as in the past, to structure their own time. Carving is something that can be done at home or incorporated into the summer camp lifestyle. It is also an activity which helps sustain the family as a cooperative working unit and educator of the young. A man does the work of finding the stone, hacking it out of the ground and transporting it back to the village to carve, not in an isolated studio, but in the kitchen, in the midst of family life, or in good weather outside, in the midst of community life. A woman helps by polishing the carvings or she may carve herself. She also dresses the skins her husband has procured and converts them into handicrafts. They teach their children. The making of arts and crafts for sale in an outside market supports the family both physically and in culturally significant ways. It is a meaningful and prestigious activity for Inuit, like hunting; an honourable way to earn one's living.

On the other hand, although it is culturally rooted and promotes the transmission of many cultural values, the production of arts and crafts for a foreign market has caused a shift in Inuit social organization. It was inevitable that inequalities should develop among carvers. The work of some sells better in the south and often, these are not the carvers most esteemed by their peers. Inuit had practised, for centuries, a natural democracy in which individual talents were recognized but not considered the basis for significant distinction. In fact, Inuit still avoid being singled out and raised above their peers. Rare is the Inuk who wittingly makes himself conspicuous among his fellows. Just because a man is a poor carver, they would say, is no reason that he should not be allowed to carve and to earn his living from it too.

Committed to maximizing good for the many, the cooperative is more able than other kinds of businesses to accommodate egalitarian attitudes. The co-op must always extend the same services and encouragement to lesser as it does to greater talents which suits Inuit just fine but is at odds with southern practise which tends to reward according to merit. Used to distinguishing talent, we, from the beginning, singled out Inuit for special regard. They used to sort themselves into better and best hunters but once linkage was made to the outside world, others began making distinctions for them — better and best students, businessmen, carvers.

The confrontation with outside priorities and standards has been met in characteristic fashion by the adaptable Inuit. Since they rely on an outside market, the most sensible thing they can do is to accede to the buyer's judgement that some carvings are better than others, even though they might continue to think otherwise. Although some of us Western folk do this, carving was never romanticized by the practical Inuit. They have always viewed it as a link to the modern world. Carvings are intended for sale in a foreign market. Their art, along with a few items of their material culture, the parka and the kayak for instance, is one of the great contributions Inuit have made to the outside world. It can be considered an attempt to balance the great volume of imported technology, making up in quality and genuineness what it may lack in quantity. Carving is a real Eskimo product, not a by-product of western know-how and it is for this reason that it is valued, by both producer and consumer and has a significant role to play in contemporary political, economic and social life of Inuit.

What future do Inuit perceive for their work? For themselves? It is sometimes thought that Inuit, lacking a concept of cause and effect, believe that the future is beyond their control. Although some are certainly, more geared to short than to long-range thinking, it should not be assumed that they do not act with an eye on results. In the past, the hunter took great care not to offend the spirits of the animals he caught. He did this to ensure future success in hunting. Now, although he often lacks useful guidelines for ensuring success in the new world, he thinks and talks a lot about the kind of future his children will have. While some Inuit scramble for position and others merely try to hold onto what they can of the old way, the more thoughtful among them are attempting to strike a balance between past and future in an ongoing effort to ground their identity and rationalize their existence.

Until recently, life was organized around the hunt and the natural leaders were men of hunting experience. Now however, there are more choices than formerly and life is organized around new priorities. Inuit may hunt but they may also be artists, craftsmen, wage labourers, politicians, or for that matter, almost anything they want. Although it is easier to live, in the physical sense at least, life is no longer

as straightforward as it was once when the necessity of finding food structured each day.

Contact has been recent and as the years go by, the old way is idealized more and more in memory, talk and art. But Inuit wouldn't go back to their former way of life any more than the rest of us would. A few years ago, people who had moved into Povungnituk from Cape Smith moved back to their old camp site which they renamed "Akulivik". There was some talk of recreating the past but whatever their intention, they succeeded in creating another town. It wasn't long before they needed houses, a school, a store, electricity. The new way of life has after all, features to recommend it. Igloos may have been remarkable structures but they were also uncomfortable and unhealthy.

Although there is nothing to be gained in attempting to regress to a glorified past, there is value in the growing movement to preserve some of the skills which served their ancestors so well and which have been pushed aside in favour of "progress". The key to mitigating some of the strain of acculturation is not a romantically inspired return to a former way of life — that never works — but rather an attempt to strike some kind of balance, incorporating the past into a future which makes sense and in which Inuit know who they are.

That is what the cultural revival is all about. Motorboats will not be replaced by kayaks and dog teams are more likely to continue participating in sportsday races than out working the land. The revival of craft techniques involves more than the production and use of things. There is a symbolic significance in the process. Materials have to be provided by the environment — sealskin, caribou, sinew and bone. This leads naturally, to a revival of at least a few aspects of the old lifestyle; a revival of the age-old interdependence of male and female work and a revival of some of the rhythms of life which used to organize time in a natural way.

The future will be decided by the young who have feet in both worlds. Some have found a more or less firm footing in the new world and are attempting to negotiate status there for other Inuit. They are balanced by others who, leaning tentatively in the opposite direction, are turning to the land

and to carving; a lifestyle which symbolizes their heritage and they hope, their future.

Notes

1. They were self-reliant but not necessarily able to continue as such. Famine and disease were taking their toll and outside intervention was probably essential to ensure physical survival.
2. This phrase is taken from a comment made by Thomas Suluk and quoted in Igalaaq (September, 1980): "Co-ops were not meant to become governments. Their main responsibility is the retail business. And as far as those co-ops in Quebec are concerned, they are more like an underground government. No question about the fact they have good roots ... just ... the question whether they should get involved in everything under the sun."
3. In 1971, Arctic Quebec cooperatives combined with the community councils to begin negotiating a form of regional government within the province of Quebec. Their efforts petered out, mainly because of federal government opposition, inaction on the part of Quebec and most telling, lack of general Inuit support. To them at that time, it was a non-issue although it has since become an issue everywhere in the north.
4. Co-op philosophy fostered aspirations towards independence and it is perhaps, not coincidental that the cooperative ideology is particularly strong among the Inuit of Arctic Quebec, a province with its own separatist inclinations.
5. Quoted in Igalaaq (May, 1980)
6. The first carvings were sold at the Canadian Guild of Crafts in Montreal.
7. In Arctic Quebec, the responsibility for arts and crafts development was completely taken over by the cooperatives when they formed a Federation in 1967 but in the Northwest Territories, it has continued as the responsibility of the government of the Northwest Territories.
8. I use "wage economy" in a general sense. Carvers are not salaried employees but are paid for each production.
9. Quoted in Igalaaq (May, 1980)
10. Although welfare programmes ensured that he was fed when his luck ran out, the distinction I am making here is that carving gave him a control over the means of production which was lacking when he had to chase after animals to eat or to trade.

Marybelle Myers
1980

190

188. AISA AMARUALI
TULUGA 1925-
Povungnituk
1953
stone
6.1 x 3.3 x 8.0
190.

189. DAVIDIALUK ALASUA
AMITTU 1910-1976
Povungnituk
1958
stone
7.0 x 14.0 x 7.0
218.

190. ANURAQ 1894-
Lake Harbour
1953
stone
8.0 x 22.3 x 22.2
258.

191

192

193

191. LUCASSIE TUKI 1935-
Inoucdjouac
1959
stone
5.5 x 6.0 x 8.5
109.

192. PEESEE OSHUITOQ 1913-1979
(OSHOOWEETOOK "A")
Cape Dorset
1958
copper
5.0 x 2.2 x 5.2
191.

193. MAKUSI QALINGO ANGUTIKIRQ 1899-
Povungnituk
1953
stone
12.0 x 18.0 x 16.5
214.

194. SILASSIE TUKI 1919-
Inoucdjouac
1957
stone and hide
21.0 x 11.5 x 18.0
105.

196. ALLIE APPAQAQ 1915-
Belcher Islands
1964
stone
4.0 x 15.0 x 13.5
223.

195. TIKITUQ QINNUAYUAK 1908-
Cape Dorset
1957
stone
9.5 x 8.0 x 4.0
102.

197. DANIEL KASUDLUAK 1925-
    Inoucdjouac
    1965
    stone
    12.0 x 6.2 x 13.0
    219.

198. SAROLIE WEETALUKTUK 1906-1962
    Inoucdjouac
    1957
    stone
    11.0 x 8.0 x 12.0
    072.

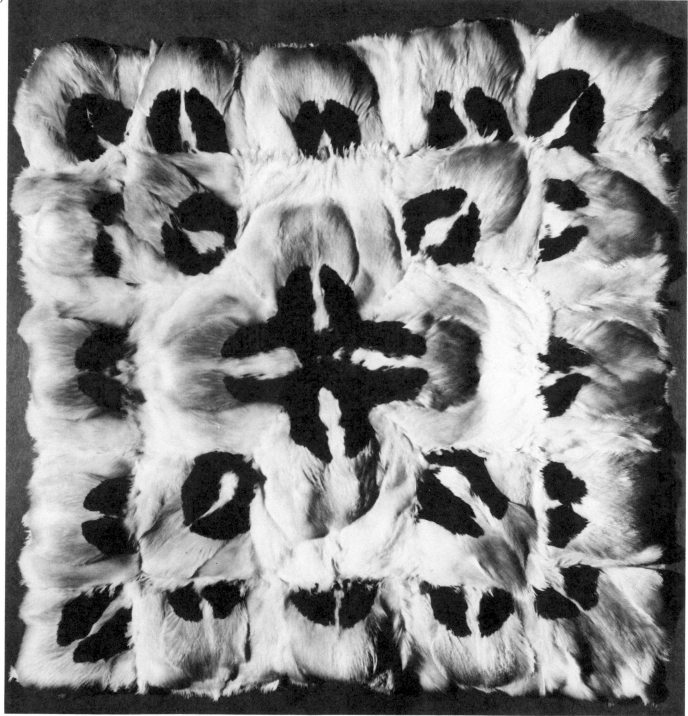

199. MAT c. 1950
      Ungava Region
      loon and eider duck
      skins
      39.0 x 41.0
      331.

200

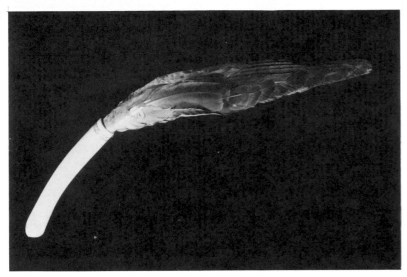

200. SNOW BRUSH c. 1953
Unidentified Artist
Cape Dorset
goose wing and ivory
58.0 x 7.5
334.

201

201. WOMAN 1979
Talligaq
Spence Bay
braided sinew,
bone and sealskin
9.2 x 5.0 x 5.0
365.

202. DOLL 1963
Lizzie Kasudluak 1914-
Inoucdjouac
fabric, hide and stone
28.0 x 17.0 x 7.2
320.

203. BIRD 1951
Sheoyuq Oqutaq 1920-
(Sheeookjuke)
Cape Dorset
sealskin and hide
7.0 x 6.0 x 17.0
318.

204. BASKET 1951
Unidentified Artist
Povungnituk
lyme grass and stone
6.5 x 22.0 x 15.5
010.

205. BAG 1951
    Unidentified Artist
    Arctic Bay
    sealskin and caribou hide
    13.0 x 10.8 x 31.0
    321.

206. MAT c. 1950
    Unidentified Artist
    Ungava Region
    loon and eider duck skins
    112.0 x 60.0
    332.

207

208

207. BASKET 1951
Unidentified Artist
Povungnituk
lyme grass, caribou teeth and ivory
7.5 x 12.0
007.

208. SPEAR HEAD c. 1900
Eastern Arctic
stone
10.5 x 3.4
290.

209

209. BASKET 1950
Unidentified Artist
Inoucdjouac
lyme grass, sealskin,
stone with soap inlay
13.0 x 26.0
004.

210. HARPOON HEAD c. 1940
Eastern Arctic
ivory and metal
9.0 x 2.5 x 1.5
055.

210

211

211. BASKET 1950
Unidentified Artist
Inoucdjouac
lyme grass and sealskin
11.8 x 20.0
005.

212

212. BASKET 1951
Unidentified Artist
Povungnituk
lyme grass, caribou teeth
and ivory
9.5 x 17.0
006.

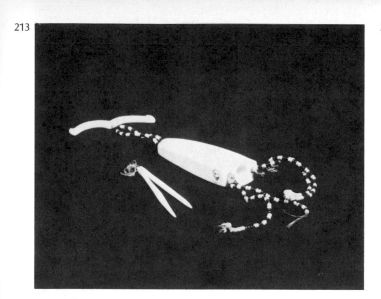

213. NEEDLE CASE c. 1900
Eastern Arctic
ivory, beads and sinew
1.8 x 24.5 x 6.0
294.

214. BASKET 1950
Unidentified Artist
Cape Smith
lyme grass and stone
7.0 x 16.5
003.

215. DRUM DANCE HAT
Date Unknown
Western Arctic
loon's beak, feathers,
caribou and ermine skins
32.0 x 20.0
343.

216. WOVEN TAPESTRY 1972
Designer: Elisapee Ishulutaq 1925-
Weaver: Oleepa Pappatsie 1952-
Pangnirtung
wool and linen warp
148.5 x 79.0
342.

217

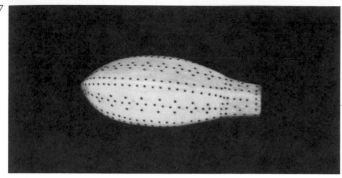

217.   TOGGLE FOR WOMAN'S GARMENT 1953
       Davidee Ningeok 1925-
       Inoucdjouac
       ivory
       2.4 x 3.5 x 9.0
       048.

218

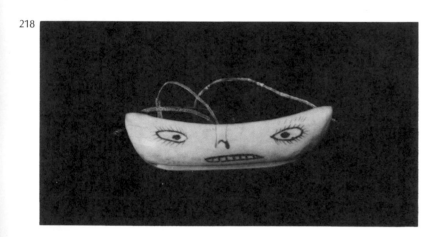

218.   SNOW GOGGLES 1953
       Makusi Qalingo Angutikirq 1899-
       Povungnituk
       bone, sinew and ink
       2.5 x 2.0 x 11.0
       293.

219

219.   BEARS TEETH c. 1930
       used as "counters"
       Unknown Area
       one tooth: 2.7 x 1.2
       047.

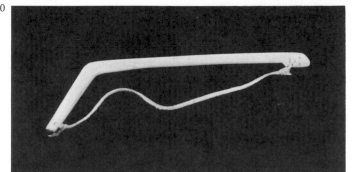

220. BOW DRILL 1953
Unidentified Artist
Eastern Arctic
bone and hide
29.2 x 2.7 x 2.0
283.

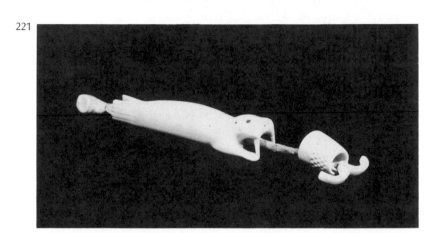

221. NEEDLE CASE 1953
Peesee Oshuitoq 1913-1979
(Oshooweetook "A")
Cape Dorset
ivory and hide
2.5 x 2.7 x 21.0
044.

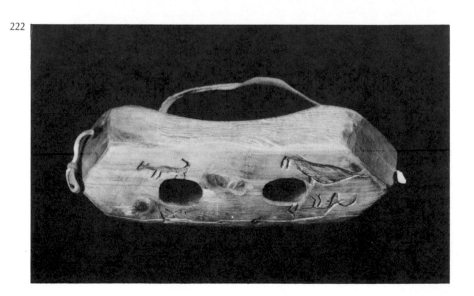

222. SNOW GOGGLES c. 1930
Eastern Arctic
wood and hide
4.0 x 5.2 x 18.0
292.

223

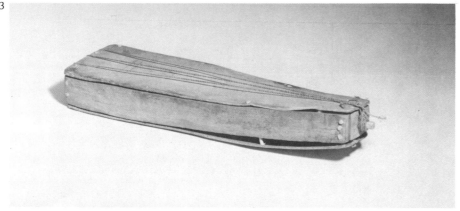

223. MUSICAL INSTRUMENT c. 1959
Peter Pitseolak 1905-1973
Cape Dorset
bone, ivory and sinew
5.5 x 11.0 x 42.5
314.

224

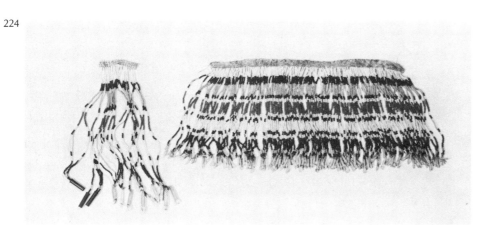

224. FRINGE FROM WOMAN'S GARMENT c. 1900
Central Arctic
beads, caribou teeth,
cartridge shells and sinew
one strand: 18.5
296.

225

225. KUDLIK (LAMP) c. 1900
Eastern Arctic
stone
8.0 x 16.5 x 36.5
264.

226. BASKET 1951
Unidentified Artist
Povungnituk
lyme grass, ivory,
stone and sealskin
8.0 x 17.5 x 14.0
009.

227. MODEL IGLOO 1940
Ungava Region
lyme grass
9.5 x 24.0 x 15.2
001.

228. HAT 1950
Ungava Region
lyme grass
10.0 x 24.0 x 28.0
002.

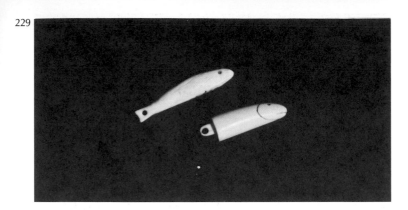

229

229A. PENDANT c. 1940
Eastern Arctic
ivory
1.0 x 0.5 x 5.0
057.

   B. PENDANT c. 1950
Eastern Arctic
ivory
1.0 x 1.0 x 4.0
056.

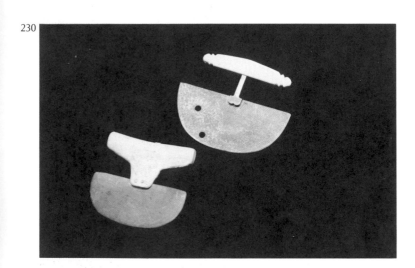

230

230A. ULU (WOMAN'S KNIFE) 1953
Tuckyashuk 1898-1972
Cape Dorset
metal and ivory
11.4 x 12.4
269.

   B. ULU c. 1900
Unknown Area
stone and bone
10.4 x 9.5
270.

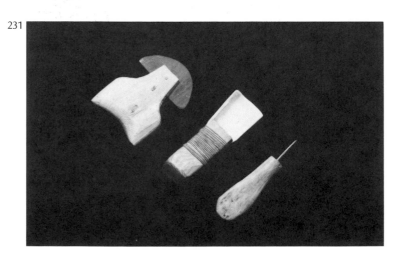

231

231A. ULU c. 1900
Unknown Area
stone and wood
10.0 x 7.3
271.

   B. SCRAPER c. 1900
Unknown Area
wood, ivory and sinew
12.2 x 4.1
272.

   C. AWL c. 1900
Unknown Area
bone and metal
11.6 x 3.4
273.

232

232. BASKET 1959
Unidentified Artist
Inoucdjouac
lyme grass and stone
8.5 x 20.5 x 15.5
011.

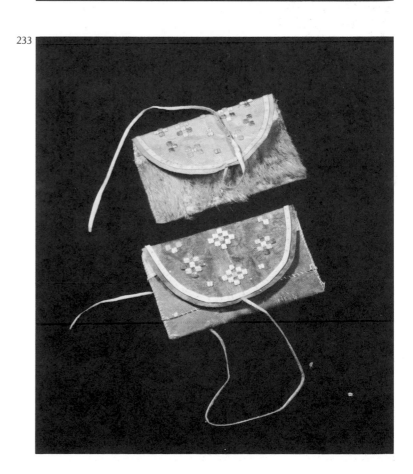
233

233. TWO POUCHES c. 1900
Greenland
sealskin, sinew and
coloured hide appliqué
7.5 x 12.0
8.0 x 12.0
291.

234

234. KUDLIK (LAMP) c. 1940
Ungava Region
stone
6.4 x 13.0 x 25.0
261.

235

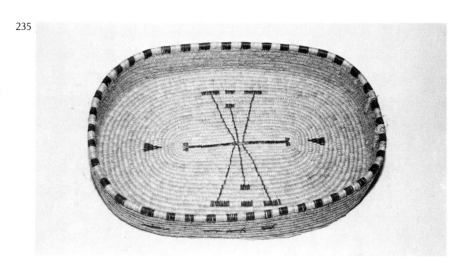

235. BASKET 1950
Unidentified Artist
Inoucdjouac
lyme grass and sealskin
12.0 x 66.0 x 44.5
012.

236

236. COOKING POT c. 1930
Eastern Arctic
stone
10.0 x 11.5 x 25.5
263.

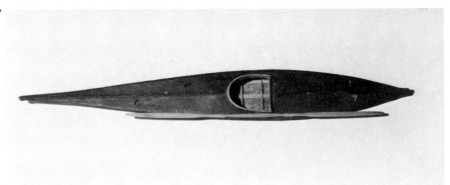

237

237. MODEL KAYAK c. 1950
Ungava Region
sealskin, wood and sinew
12.0 x 85.0
336.

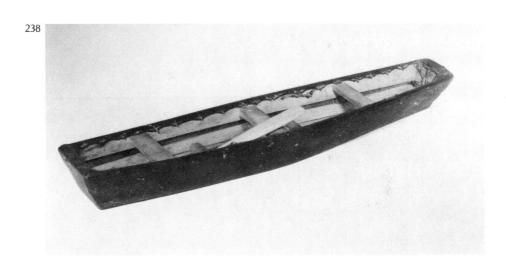

238

238. MODEL UMIAQ (BOAT) c. 1950
Ungava Region
sealskin, wood and sinew
6.0 x 13.5 x 50.0
316.

239

239. MODEL KUDLIK 1963
Paulosie Paulosie 1915-
Inoucdjouac
stone, ivory and sinew
12.5 x 18.5 x 12.0
260.

240. CUP c. 1930.
Ungava Region
stone
3.5 x 5.9 x 8.0
262.

241. PATTERN ILLUSTRATION 1950
Ungava Region
sealskin appliqué on
bleached caribou hide
18.3 x 36.4
333.

242. DOLL c. 1950
Unknown Area
sealskin, ivory and hide
22.2 x 8.0 x 3.5
319.

243

243. BELT c. 1900
Greenland
sealskin, sinew and
coloured hide appliqué
6.4 x 33.5
322.

244

244. BAG 1951
Oodluriak 1924-1971
Cape Dorset
sealskin, caribou hide,
beads, ivory and sinew
35.5 x 42.0
323.

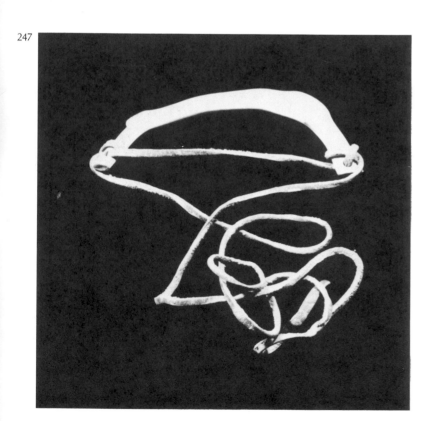

245. BASKET 1951
    Unidentified Artist
    Povungnituk
    lyme grass, ivory and stone
    10.5 x 18.0
    008.

246. SCRAPER 1960
    Peter Pitseolak 1900-1973
    Cape Dorset
    stone
    18.5 x 8.7
    280.

247. FISH JIGGER date unknown
    Unknown Area
    bone and hide
    2.1 x 23.4
    279.

248

248. APPLIQUE c. 1950
Ungava Region
bleached caribou
hide on sealskin
24.0 x 22.7
328.

249. DAVID TUKTUDYUK 1946-
    Repulse Bay
    1967
    ivory
    7.0 x 7.5 x 2.3
    129.

250. PEESEE OSHUITOQ 1913-1979
    (OSHOOWEETOOK "A")
    Cape Dorset
    1953
    stone and ink
    5.5 x 5.5 x 3.0
    015.

251. LUCASSIE USUIKTUAYUK 1897-1962
    Sugluk
    1959
    stone
    7.5 x 12.0 x 9.0
    251.

252

252. PEESEE OSHUITOQ 1913-1979
(OSHOOWEETOOK "A")
Cape Dorset
1953
stone and ivory
11.0 x 6.0 x 3.5
046.

253. SAROLIE WEETALUKTUK 1906-1962
Inoucdjouac
1953
ivory
3.0 x 1.5 x 28.0
034.

254. ANURAQ 1894-
Lake Harbour
1960
ivory
4.5 x 3.0 x 8.0
017.

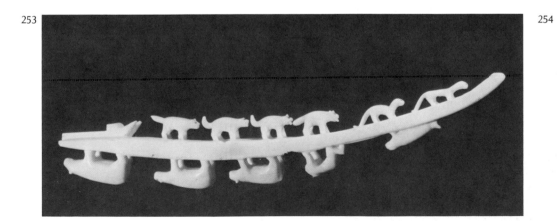

253

254

255. KIAKSHUK 1886-1967
Cape Dorset
1963
stone
20.0 x 11.0 x 9.7
338.

256

257

258

256. SAMWILLIE IQALUQ 1925-
    Belcher Islands
    1964
    stone
    7.2 x 3.3 x 10.2
    234.

257. JOHNASSIE TOOKALUK 1912-
    Belcher Islands
    1964
    stone
    5.0 x 6.0 x 10.5
    238.

258. SAMWILLIE IQALUQ 1925-
    Belcher Islands
    1964
    stone
    7.5 x 14.1 x 8.5
    229.

259. KIAWAK ASHOONA 1933-
    (KIUGAK)
    Cape Dorset
    1962
    stone
    29.0 x 11.0 x 20.0
    156.

260. AISA QUMA IGAUJA 1915-
(AISAPIK POV)
Povungnituk
1958
stone and hide
8.4 x 6.0 x 15.0
093.

261. ALICE TOOKTOO 1947-
Great Whale River
1978
stone and ivory
7.0 x 9.0 x 5.3
362.

262. CHARLIE PANIGONIAK 1946-
Rankin Inlet
1972
stone and bone
10.0 x 14.0 x 9.5
082.

263

264

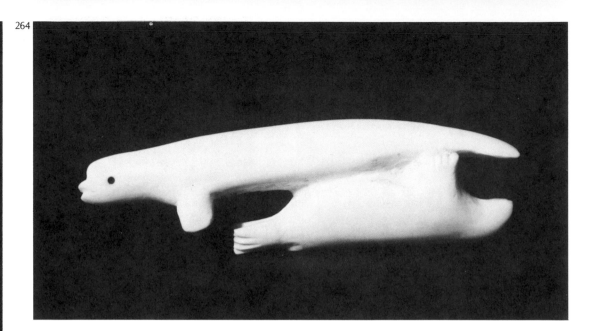

264. EASTERN ARCTIC c. 1930
ivory
2.3 x 3.5 x 11.0
045.

263. KILIKTEE
Lake Harbour
1960
bone
21.0 x 6.5 x 4.0
139.

265. CHARLIE SIVUARAPIK 1911-1968
    (SHEGOAPIK)
    Povungnituk
    1953
    ivory
    2.8 x 3.2 x 3.5
    023.

266. CHARLIE SIVUARAPIK 1911-1968
    (SHEGOAPIK)
    Povungnituk
    1953
    ivory
    6.0 x 3.1 x 11.2
    014.

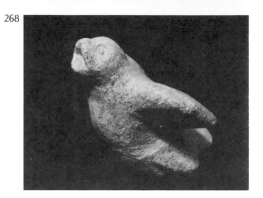

267. UNIDENTIFIED ARTIST
Inoucdjouac
c. 1952
stone and ivory
11.0 x 6.0 x 7.5
076.

268. MARY ADLOOK 1928-
Payne Bay
1960
stone
7.0 x 6.5 x 5.0
232.

269. ANGATUK NASSAK 1931-
Payne Bay
1960
stone
11.0 x 4.5 x 3.3
101.

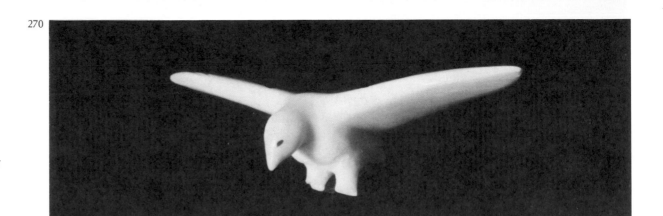

270. UNIDENTIFIED ARTIST
Cape Dorset
1957
ivory
2.0 x 6.5 x 3.0
054.

271. NALENIK TEMELA 1929-
Lake Harbour
1960
ivory and stone
10.3 x 7.0 x 6.4
032.

272

273

274

275

272. SAROLIE WEETALUKTUK 1906-1962
Inoucdjouac
1959
stone
24.0 x 10.5 x 5.5
136.

273. LUCASSIE TAKATAK 1942-
Belcher Islands
1964
stone
5.0 x 9.0 x 14.1
222.

274. DANIEL KASUDLUAK 1925-
Inoucdjouac
1965
stone
6.1 x 5.3 x 18.0
181.

275. MADELEINE ISSERKUT 1928-
Repulse Bay
1965
stone and ivory
15.0 x 4.5 x 15.0
195.

276. SHEOYUQ OQUTAQ 1920-
     (SHEEOOKJUKE)
     Cape Dorset
     1968
     stone and ivory
     4.0 x 16.5 x 16.5
     123.

277. AXANGAYUK SHAA 1937-
     (AQJANGAJUK)
     Cape Dorset
     1958
     stone
     19.0 x 8.5 x 22.0
     201.

278. PUDLAT POOTOOGOOK 1919-
Cape Dorset
1964
stone
9.0 x 7.0 x 14.1
221.

279. UNIDENTIFIED ARTIST
Povungnituk
1955
stone and ivory
8.0 x 6.5 x 17.0
178.

280. UNIDENTIFIED ARTIST
Povungnituk
1955
stone and ivory
14.5 x 17.0 x 32.0
311.

281. ETOSACK SAMSACK 1916-
  Inoucdjouac
  1951
  stone and ivory
  8.0 x 3.0 x 5.0
  210.

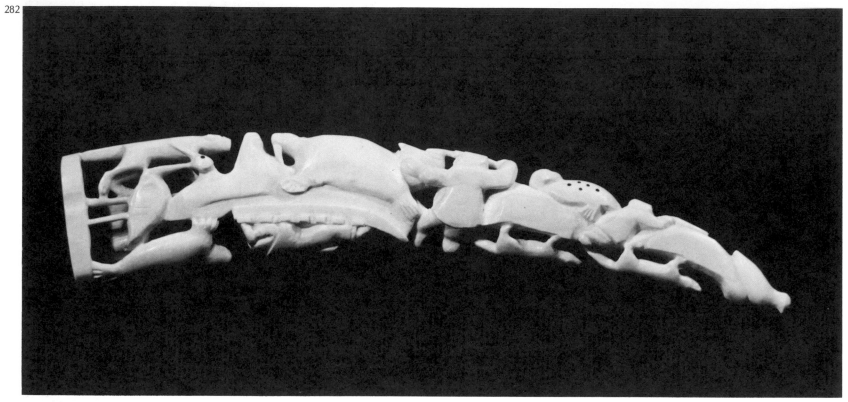

282. SAROLIE WEETALUKTUK 1906-1962
Inoucdjouac
1960
ivory
5.2 x 27.0 x 3.0
022.

283

283. TIVI PANINGAJAK 1917-
Povungnituk
1953
ivory and stone
2.7 x 3.6 x 3.5
043.

284

284. MADELEINE ISSERKUT 1928-
Repulse Bay
1960
ivory and bone
7.5 x 5.5 x 9.5
031.

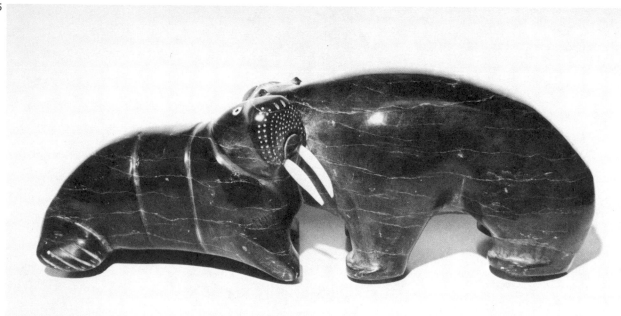

285. 2 views
ELIJASSIAPIK 1912-
Inoucdjouac
stone and ivory
12.0 x 11.2 x 34.0
300.

286. OTTOCHIE ASHOONA
1942-1970
Cape Dorset
1962
stone
19.0 x 21.5 x 9.6
067

287. UNIDENTIFIED ARTIST
Great Whale River
1959
stone and ivory
9.5 x 5.5 x 40.0
303.

288. 2 views
AISA AMARUALI TULUGA 1925-
(ISA TOOL)
Povungnituk
1953
stone and ivory
8.5 x 4.3 x 5.5
088.

289. TIKITUQ QINNUAYUAK 1908-
Cape Dorset
1956
stone, calcite and ink
5.5 x 10.8 x 15.0
168.

290. PARSA NOWRA 1930-
Great Whale River
1978
stone and ivory
24.0 x 13.5 x 4.5
361.

293

291. JOHNNY INNUPPA QUMALU 1937-
Povungnituk
1961
stone
11.5 x 8.5 x 2.6
111.

292. LUCASSIE NOWYA 1924-
Great Whale River
1959
stone
6.5 x 4.5 x 15.0
243.

293. LUCASSIE KUMARLUK 1921-
Inoucdjouac
1961
stone
13.0 x 5.0 x 11.2
220.

294. PAULOSIE PAULOSIE 1915-
Inoucdjouac
1961
stone and ivory
10.5 x 7.0 x 19.0
205.

295
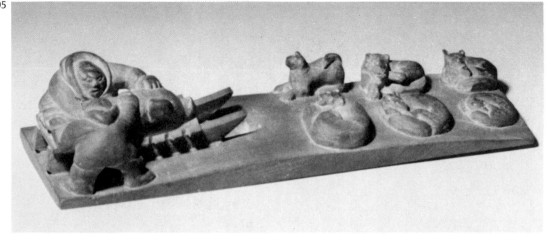

295. ISA KASUDLUAK 1917-
Inoucdjouac
1958
stone
5.5 x 7.0 x 24.5
121.

296

296. MARK TUNGILIK 1913-
Repulse Bay
1961
stone
9.0 x 13.0 x 4.0
249.

297. LUKASI TUKALA 1917-
Povungnituk
1958
stone
16.5 x 20.0 x 14.0
126.

298. SIMEONIE KINGALIK 1930-
Inoucdjouac
1953
stone and ivory
9.0 x 6.0 x 6.5
091.

299. SAKKEASSIE RAGEE 1924-
Cape Dorset
1965
stone
5.0 x 4.5 x 9.5
226.

300. UNIDENTIFIED ARTIST
Povungnituk
1957
stone
20.0 x 14.0 x 24.0
132.

301. SAROLIE WEETALUKTUK 1906-1962
Inoucdjouac
1955
stone
20.0 x 13.0 x 13.0
127.

302. UNIDENTIFIED ARTIST
Inoucdjouac
1954
stone and ivory
9.2 x 5.0 x 3.1
211.

303. ELIJASSIAPIK 1912-
Inoucdjouac
1953
stone and ivory
6.5 x 8.0 x 32.0
309.

304. SHOONAGAROO KOOTOOK 1936-
Spence Bay
1971
whale bone and ivory
28.0 x 11.5 x 5.5
053.

305. MAKUSI QALINGO ANGUTIKIRQ 1899-
Povungnituk
1953
stone, ivory and hide
8.0 x 5.5 x 18.0
304.

305

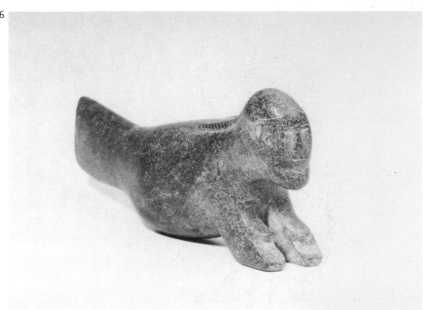

306. LATCHAULASSIE AKESUK 1919-
Cape Dorset
1956
stone
6.5 x 3.0 x 16.0
145.

307. UNIDENTIFIED ARTIST
Cape Dorset
1961
stone
11.0 x 18.0 x 33.0
154.

308. MOSES APPAQAQ 1926-
Belcher Islands
1964
stone
8.5 x 13.0 x 8.5
237.

309. KUMWARTOK ASHOONA 1930-
Cape Dorset
1980
stone
11.5 x 21.0 x 5.5
369.

311. MUNGITOK 1940-
    Cape Dorset
    "Man Carried To The Moon"
    stonecut No. 21/1959
    Cape Dorset catalogue
    345.

310. LUKTA QIATSUK 1928-
    Cape Dorset
    "Talluliyuk"
    stonecut No. 23/1959
    Cape Dorset catalogue
    344.

312. NOT ILLUSTRATED
    MUNGITOK 1940-
    Cape Dorset
    "Man Carried To The Moon"
    stone rubbing No. 24/1959
    Cape Dorset catalogue
    346.

Unidentified Artist
Eastern Arctic
Bear's Head and Whale 1953
ivory and stone
5.5 x 4.0 x 2.5
025.

Unidentified Artist
Inoucdjouac
Bird 1953
ivory
3.0 x 5.0 x 4.5
037.

Unidentified Artist
Repulse Bay
Whale 1953
ivory
2.5 x 1.8 x 6.0
038.

Unidentified Artist
Repulse Bay
Bird 1959
ivory
4.0 x 2.5 x 6.0
040.

Donat Milortok 1942-
Repulse Bay
Bird 1968
ivory
2.5 x 1.0 x 5.0
042.

Unidentified Artist
Eastern Arctic
Finger Ring c.1950
ivory
1.3 diameter
058.

Unidentified Artist
Inoucdjouac
Two Hunters and Whale 1949
stone
17.0 x 30.0 x 12.0
097.

Alasua Tamusi Nutaraalu 1930-
Povungnituk
Unfinished Carving of a Man 1959
stone
10.0 x 10.0 x 19.2
135.

Unidentified Artist
Lake Harbour
Bird 1957
stone
5.0 x 2.3 x 6.6
216.

Samuellee Iqaluq 1925-
(Echalook)
Belcher Islands
Bird 1964
stone
6.4 x 3.8 x 8.5
224.

Unidentified Artist
Great Whale River
Bird 1959
stone
9.0 x 4.5 x 17.0
225.

Paulosie Kasudluak 1928-
Inoucdjouac
Bird 1959
stone
6.0 x 3.5 x 11.0
231.

Philiposie Napartuk 1931-
Inoucdjouac
Whale 1953
stone
6.5 x 3.0 x 12.0
256.

Paulosie Paulosie 1915-
Inoucdjouac
Kudlik (Lamp) 1959
stone
4.5 x 8.3 x 16.0
259.

Unidentified Artist
Belcher Islands
Ulu 1955
stone 9.5 x 11.5
265.

Ungava Region
Four Spear Heads c.1900
stone
15.0 x 6.5
7.7 x 3.5
6.0 x 1.5
6.3 x 3.6
266. 267. 268A. 268B.

Ungava Region
Unidentified Artifact c.1900
bone 30.0 x 2.0
274.

Unidentified Artist
Ungava Region
Knife 1952
bone
21.2 x 1.6
275.

Unidentified Artist
Belcher Islands
Ulu 1955
stone
7.3 x 12.5
277.

Ungava Region
Knife c.1940
ivory, wood and sinew
23.4 x 2.1
278.

Ungava Region
Cross Bow (Model) 1952
wood and sinew
18.0 x 17.5 x 2.2
281.

Ungava Region
Cross Bow (Model) 1952
wood and sinew
17.2 x 16.0 x 2.2
282.

Ungava Region
Spinning Game, date unknown
bone, wood and sinew
length 51.0
284.

Ungava Region
Barbed Arrow Head c.1900
bone
22.6 x 1.0
286.

Ungava Region
Drill c.1900
bone
15.0 x 0.8
287.

Ungava Region
Toggle for Dog Harness c.1900
bone
5.5 x 3.2
288.

Unidentified Artist
Baker Lake
Bucket and Dipper (Model) 1965
caribou hide and ivory
4.0 x 9.5 x 5.0
295.

Lucie Angalakte 1931-
Repulse Bay
Man and Kayak 1965
stone and ivory
6.5 x 3.2 x 18.0
306.

Kapik Kolola 1926-
Lake Harbour
Man and Kayak 1962
stone and ivory
6.7 x 4.0 x 25.2
307.

Mark Tungilik 1913-
Repulse Bay
Man and Kayak 1961
bone and ivory
6.0 x 3.2 x 16.0
308.

Johnny Inukpuk 1930-
Inoucdjouac
Walrus 1955
stone and ivory
11.0 x 14.2 x 23.3
313.

Ungava Region
Arrow Case 1949
sealskin and ivory
74.0 x 12.0
315.

Ungava Region
Kayak Model c.1949
seal hide and wood
94.0 x 11.6 x 3.0
317.

Greenland
Slippers early 20th C.
hide
length: 26.0
324.

Labrador
Long Boots c.1930
sealskin and cotton fabric
height: 39.5
325.

Ungava Region
Women, Children and Igloo c.1950
sealskin appliqué on caribou hide
16.3 x 17.5
326.

Ungava Region
Family c.1950
sealskin appliqué on caribou hide
33.0 x 30.0
327.

Ungava Region
Children and Animals c.1950
sealskin appliqué on caribou hide
19.5 x 26.5
329.

Ungava Region
Men, Women and Birds c.1950
sealskin appliqué on caribou hide
15.3 x 28.0
330.

Unidentified Artist
Inoucdjouac
Two Dolls 1963
stone, fabric and lyme grass
21.5 x 30.5 x 15.0
335.

Ungava Region
Model Boat with
Sails and Paddles c. 1950
hide, skin and wood
6.0 x 18.5
337.

Unidentified Artist
Inoucdjouac
Man and Spear 1953
stone and ivory
16.5 x 30.0 x 11.0
339.

Western Arctic
Man and Kayak c. 1900
hide, skin and wood
13.5 x 11.0 x 67.0
355.

PRINTS

Pootoogook 1887-c. 1959
and Kanaginak 1935-
Cape Dorset
"Legend of the Blind Man
And The Bear"
stencil No. 5/1959
Cape Dorset catalogue
347.

Kanaginak 1935-
Cape Dorset
"Summer Caribou"
engraving No. 2/1973
Cape Dorset catalogue
349.

Angosaglo 1895-
(Anguhadluq)
Baker Lake
"Animals"
stencil No. 22/1970
Baker Lake catalogue
350.

Tivi Etook 1928-
George River
"Dance of the Hares"
stonecut No. 6/1975
Tivi Etook catalogue
351.

Levi Kumaluk 1919-
(Qumaluk)
Povungnituk
"Emerging Seal"
stencil No. 10/1972
Arctic Quebec catalogue
352.